BRIDESHEAD REVISITED

The Past Redeemed

TWAYNE'S MASTERWORK STUDIES

Robert Lecker, General Editor

BRIDESHEAD REVISITED

The Past Redeemed

Robert Murray Davis

TWAYNE PUBLISHERS • BOSTON
A Division of G. K. Hall & Co.

Twayne's Masterwork Studies No. 59

Copyright 1990 by G. K. Hall & Co.
All rights reserved.
Published by Twayne Publishers
A division of G. K. Hall & Co.
70 Lincoln Street
Boston, Massachusetts 02111

Copyediting supervised by Barbara Sutton.
Book production by Janet Z. Reynolds.
Typeset by Huron Valley Graphics, Ann Arbor, Michigan.

First published 1990.
10 9 8 7 6 5 4 3 2 1 (hc)
10 9 8 7 6 5 4 3 2 1 (pb)

Library of Congress Cataloging-in-Publication Data
Davis, Robert Murray.
Brideshead revisited : the past redeemed / Robert Murray Davis.
p.   cm. — (Twayne's masterwork studies ; no. 59)
Includes bibliographical references (p.   ) and index.
ISBN 0-8057-8092-0 (alk. paper). — ISBN 0-8057-8138-2 (pbk. :
alk. paper)
1. Waugh, Evelyn, 1903–1966.   Brideshead revisited.   I. Title.
II. Series.
PR6045.A97B734   1990
823'.912—dc20   90-4636
                                                      CIP

Contents

Note on the References
and Acknowledgments

Brideshead Revisited has an extraordinarily complicated textual history, which I trace in some detail in my *Evelyn Waugh, Writer* (Norman, Okla.: Pilgrim Books, 1981). Waugh's American publisher, Little, Brown, however, has issued only one version of the text, in 1946 and subsequently, both in cloth and paperback editions. It contains two obvious errors: "flash," on page 95, line 21, should read "flask"; and "thread," on page 327, line 33, should read "threat."

Waugh made minor revisions to English editions through the Uniform Edition, published by Chapman and Hall in 1949, and ten years later he made more extensive revisions, tending to cut rather than rewrite, for the edition published by Chapman and Hall in 1960.

For this study I have used the Little, Brown edition, with page references cited parenthetically. Excerpts from *Brideshead Revisited* by Evelyn Waugh, copyright 1944, 1945 by Evelyn Waugh; © renewed 1972, 1973 by Mrs. Laura Waugh, are reprinted by permission of Little, Brown & Co.

All of the critics who have written about Waugh, including many not cited in the notes and bibliography, have helped me to discover my own views. Donat Gallagher has given me material that I would not otherwise have discovered. Paul A. Doyle and Donald Greene shared with me the results of their extensive study of the allusions and the historical background to the text. Jeanette Gregory Harris acted as consultant on points of style, sense, and grammar.

Evelyn Waugh
Photograph by Howard Coster, F.R.S.A. Used with the permission of Mr. Auberon Waugh.

Chronology:
Evelyn Waugh's
Life and Works

Bracketed material dates fictional events in *Brideshead Revisited*.

1898   Alexander Raban Waugh born, first son of Arthur Waugh, director of Chapman and Hall Publishing Company and man of letters, and Catherine Raban Waugh.

1900   [Lord Brideshead born, eldest son of Lord Marchmain.]

1901   Queen Victoria dies; King Edward VII accedes to throne.

1903   [Charles Ryder born in October; Sebastian Flyte born on unspecified date.] Arthur Evelyn St. John Waugh, second of two children, born 28 October.

1905   [Lady Julia Flyte born.]

1910   Evelyn enters Heath Mount School. Publishes privately an opposition paper, "The Cynic," and a religious poem, "The World to Come" (both published in 1916).

1911   [Lady Cordelia Flyte born.]

1914   World War I begins.

1917   Publication of brother Alec's *The Loom of Youth*, considered an attack on Sherborne, Alec and Arthur's public school. Waugh sent instead to Lancing in May. After an unpromising beginning, becomes founder of Dilettanti and Corpse Club, house-captain, editor of the school magazine, president of debating society; wins prizes for verse, prose, and drawing.

1922   Enters Hertford College, Oxford, on history scholarship in January. Joins Oxford Union Debating Society; writes and draws for undergraduate journals; leads an increasingly dissolute life. [Charles Ryder and Lord Sebastian Flyte matriculate at Oxford in October.]

1923   [Action of *Brideshead Revisited* begins.]

1924	Receives a Third on his examinations but leaves Oxford without taking a degree. Enters Heatherley's Art School; ignores studies for parties in Oxford and London. Writes script for and appears in *The Scarlet Woman*, an amateur film. [Sebastian sent down from Oxford; to the Levant with Mr. Samgrass. Charles leaves Oxford to study art in Paris.]
1925	Master at Arnold House, Denbighshire. Begins draft of first professional story, "The Balance," (published 1926); attempts suicide by swimming out to sea, but is deterred by jellyfish stings. Master at Aston Clinton and elsewhere. [Lady Julia Flyte marries Rex Mottram.]
1926	May, General Strike in which Waugh [and Charles Ryder] play minor roles. Publishes, privately, *P. R. B. An Essay on the Pre-Raphaelite Brotherhood*. Fired from Aston Clinton. [Lady Marchmain dies. Charles receives first commission for paintings of Marchmain House.]
1927	Abortive apprenticeship with *Daily Express;* commissioned to write centenary biography of Dante Gabriel Rossetti; meets Evelyn Gardner; begins *Decline and Fall*.
1928	Publishes *Rossetti* in April; marries Evelyn Gardner in June; publishes *Decline and Fall* in September.
1929	Belated honeymoon to Mediterranean marred by wife's illness. Returns home to write *Labels* (in America *A Bachelor Abroad*), his first travel book, and *Vile Bodies* (both published in 1930). Wife leaves him for John Heygate in July.
1930	Divorce is granted in January. *Vile Bodies* is a best-seller, making Waugh a social as well as a literary success. Writes series of articles for the *Daily Mail;* book page in *Graphic*. Converts to Roman Catholicism in September. Travels to Abyssinia for coronation of Haile Selassie (dispatches published in *Times*), and to Aden, Kenya, and South Africa (October–February 1931). [Charles marries Lady Celia and has first exhibition of paintings.]
1931	Writes *Remote People* (in America as *They Were Still Dancing*) and *Black Mischief* (published in 1932). Meets Lady Diana Cooper. Proposes to Teresa Jungman; is refused.
1932	Travels to British Guiana (December).
1933	Returns to England in May. Writes but does not publish "An Open Letter to His Eminence the Cardinal Archbishop of Westminster" responding to attacks on *Black Mischief* by the editor of the *Tablet*. Meets Laura Herbert, a first cousin of Evelyn Gardner.

1934	Travels to Fez, Morocco, to write *A Handful of Dust. Ninety-two Days* (travel); *A Handful of Dust*. Makes expedition to Spitzbergen. [Charles discovers Celia's infidelity and goes to Latin America to paint.]
1935	*Edmund Campion* wins Hawthornden Prize. Travels to Ethiopia as war correspondent for the *Daily Mail*.
1936	Returns to Ethiopia to gather material for book about the war. Marriage to Evelyn Gardner is annulled. *Mr. Loveday's Little Outing and Other Sad Stories. Waugh in Abyssinia*. [Charles and Julia begin their affair aboard ship—even though Julia has not yet turned thirty. Charles's exhibition.] Crisis over King Edward VIII's infatuation with Mrs. Simpson.
1937	Marries Laura Herbert 17 April and settles at Piers Court in Gloucester. Writes weekly book reviews for *Night and Day*, July–December. First collected edition of his novels.
1938	*Scoop*. Maria Theresa, first of four daughters, born. Travels to Mexico, financed by English oil interests wishing to influence English public opinion about expropriation of their holdings, resulting in *Robbery under Law* (in America, *Mexico: An Object Lesson;* both 1939). Neville Chamberlain signs agreement with Adolf Hitler at Munich. [Lord Brideshead announces his engagement to Beryl Muspratt.]
1939	[Lord Marchmain returns to England, winter; dies in summer.] Auberon Alexander, first of three sons, born. World War II declared 1 September. Waugh abandons *Work Suspended* (published as fragment in 1942) to join Royal Marines.
1940	Sails to Dakar for abortive invasion. Transfers to Commandos. Daughter Mary dies one day after birth.
1941	Goes to Egypt with Robert Laycock's battalion; sees action on North African coast; lands on Crete and retreats across the island in May. Reassigned to Royal Marines; returns to England by ship, writing *Put Out More Flags* (1942) en route.
1942	Transferred to Special Services. Assigned to various training schools and military posts; denied combat assignments. Daughter Margaret born. [Charles Ryder is thirty-nine.]
1943	Father dies. Resigns from Special Services. Visits deathbed of Hubert Duggan and induces the family to call a priest. Cracks bone in leg while parachuting. [Charles Ryder returns to Brideshead.]
1944	Secures leave to write *Brideshead Revisited*, January–June. Daughter Harriet born. Assigned to British Mission in Yugoslavia under command of Randolph Churchill. Privately issued

version of *Brideshead. Brideshead* serialized, with cuts not authorized by Waugh, in *Town and Country* (November–February 1945).

1945   Has audience with Pope Pius XII about situation of Croatian Catholics under Tito. Returns to England in March. *Brideshead* published 28 May to mixed reviews; some prominent critics attack it on grounds of its supposed religious or social snobbery. Returns with family to Piers Court, which had been rented to a convent, and in September is discharged from military service. Begins *Helena.*

1946   Travels, first to Spain and then to Nuremburg for war crimes trials. *When the Going Was Good* (selections from travel books). *Brideshead* is a best-seller in United States. Son James born.

1947   *Wine in Peace and War.* Travels to Hollywood to discuss film rights to *Brideshead;* spends most of time at Forest Lawn Cemetery. Writes "Death in Hollywood" (*Life,* September) and articles critical of movie studios (*Daily Telegraph,* April–May). Travels to Scandinavia for *Daily Telegraph. Scott-King's Modern Europe.* Decides against emigrating to Ireland.

1948   *The Loved One. Work Suspended and Other Stories Written before the Second World War.* Lectures on G. K. Chesterton, Ronald Knox, and Graham Greene to Catholic audiences in United States and gathers material for essay on American Catholic Church (*Life,* September 1949).

1949   "The Major Intervenes," story later adapted as climactic episode of war trilogy.

1950   Son Septimus born. *Helena.*

1951   Travels to Middle East, gathering material for essay on the Holy Places (*Life,* December).

1952   *The Holy Places. Men at Arms,* first volume of *Sword of Honour* trilogy. Joins Catholic and conservative agitation against visit of Tito to England through March 1953. Travels to Goa.

1953   *Love among the Ruins.* Controversy with Hugh Trevor-Roper on Sir/St. Thomas More.

1954   Suffers delusions from bromide poisoning while en route to Ceylon. *Tactical Exercise* (American collection of stories). Mother dies.

1955   *Officers and Gentlemen,* second volume of *Sword of Honour.* Controversy with Nancy Spain, whose unannounced visit to

Piers Court he had repulsed. Involved with Nancy Mitford in a discussion of language and class.

1956   Wins libel suits against *Daily Express* and Nancy Spain. Sells Piers Court; moves to Combe Florey, Taunton, Somerset.

1957   *The Ordeal of Gilbert Pinfold.* Ronald Knox dies; Waugh named literary executor and official biographer; occupied with these duties through 1959.

1958   *The World of Evelyn Waugh,* anthology.

1959   *The Life of the Right Reverend Ronald Knox.* Revises and cuts *Brideshead* and adds preface for first volume of Uniform Edition (1960 and following). Refuses to accept the honor of Commander of the British Empire.

1960   *A Tourist in Africa,* last travel book, which he terms a potboiler. Writes series of travel articles on Europe, "Passport into Spring," for *Daily Mail.* BBC interview with John Freeman.

1961   *Unconditional Surrender* (in America *The End of the Battle*), final volume of *Sword of Honour* trilogy.

1963   Becomes Companion of Literature. *Basil Seal Rides Again.* Expresses dismay in articles and letters to magazines at changes in Roman Catholic liturgy and practice brought about by Second Vatican Council.

1964   *A Little Learning,* autobiography to 1925. Projected second volume abandoned after a few pages.

1965   *Sword of Honour* slightly abridged in one volume.

1966   Dies at home 10 April after hearing Easter Mass in Latin.

1

Historical Context

Evelyn Waugh cannot be securely placed in the tradition of the realistic novel that dominated critical opinion and popular taste during his youth in the early years of this century, but his novels did reflect, farcically but with surprising accuracy as far as they went, not only his personal history but significant aspects of the social history of his time.

The milieu in which he grew up was significantly different from that of the realists and even more different from that of major modernist writers—like James Joyce, Joseph Conrad, T. S. Eliot, and D. H. Lawrence—who achieved dominant positions in the first three decades of the twentieth century and have held them ever since. Only Lawrence was English by birth, and he was the son of a coal miner, raised outside the Establishment pattern of public school (in England a very different and far more exclusive category than in the United States) and university education, which until recently meant education at Oxford or Cambridge University.

Although Waugh inserted at the beginning of *Brideshead Revisited* an "Author's Note" insisting "I am not I; thou art not he or she; they are not they," Charles Ryder's background is a convenient point of reference in describing Waugh's background. Waugh's family was more definitely placed in the suburban middle class and somewhat less well off than Charles Ryder's. Waugh, like his narrator John Plant in *Work Suspended*, belonged to "the moneyless, landless, educated gentry who managed the country" for the Establishment,[1] whereas Ryder's uncle has something like a country estate. Charles's father clearly has inherited income, whereas Arthur Waugh was a salaried employee, even if he was managing director, of a publishing house. Unlike Charles, Waugh complained not of his father's eccentricity but of his utter conventionality in literary taste (liked Kipling; hated T. S. Eliot) and social behavior; his mother survived well past the publication of *Brideshead Revisited*. As a child Waugh had a sound Church of England training and a fervent or at least an ostentatious faith; and though he probably wished at times to be an only child, he had an elder brother, Alec, whose athletic, literary, and amorous feats he disparaged and envied until the late 1920s.

On the other hand, author and character shared major elements in personal, social, and intellectual history. Both were born in October 1903, which means that they experienced ten years of Edwardian economic and social security before it was shattered by the outbreak of World War I. Both reveled in the idyllic freedom of Oxford—Waugh said that he regarded his scholarship as a reward of work already done rather than as an incentive to further study—and in being accepted into social and intellectual circles, represented in the novel by Sebastian Flyte and Anthony Blanche, entirely new and very seductive. Both attained technical mastery of their respective arts and a degree of popular acclaim and financial success in the 1930s, though Charles Ryder's path was more direct and his art more closely linked to monuments and styles from the English past than, until *Brideshead Revisited*, Waugh's had been.

Waugh did not ally himself with avant-garde writing. Brought up as the son of a publisher and minor literary man, he had a solid grounding in English poetry and fiction but very little knowledge of continental writers and movements. Charles Ryder's list of "meagre and commonplace" books (27) represents fairly enough Waugh's tastes: the volumes of *Georgian Poetry* were consciously middle-of-the-road; A. E. Housman's *A Shropshire Lad* and Compton Mackenzie's *Sinister Street* (which included a portrait of Oxford dear to the young Waugh's imagination) represented a break with Victorian forms in rather sentimentalized and hardly revolutionary fashion; and Lytton Strachey's *Eminent Victorians* and Norman Douglas's *South Wind* undercut conventional values in a stylish and indeed stylized fashion.

These writers might have been considered "advanced," but they were hardly avant-garde. Waugh—and Charles—came up to Oxford in 1922, the year in which James Joyce's *Ulysses* and T. S. Eliot's *The Waste Land* were published. Anthony Blanche, who reads Aldous Huxley's newly published *Antic Hay* and declaims *The Waste Land* to passing undergraduates, is Charles's link to experimental literature and to current fashions in art. But even he is a consumer rather than a producer.

These and other, less obvious, allusions help to place the novel firmly in its period, and even hostile critics have testified to the accuracy with which it presents the milieu of Oxford in 1923. But the novel does not reflect Waugh's sense that he was part of a new generation which, because of the shift in political and social values occasioned by World War I, was unprecedented and perhaps unique. Like Boy Mulcaster and Charles (205) he regretted missing active service, but he scorned the generation who brought about the war and resented, not at all unconsciously, those who had returned from combat to dominate the world he hoped to enter. Waugh developed very early and very consciously a sense that his period—he preferred the term "generation"—was different.

Although he made an early reputation writing about the problems and promise of "Youth," he differed from the revolutionaries of the American 1960s in finding the younger generation no wiser or more effective than its predecessors and in calling for self-discipline and responsibility along traditional lines rather than more freedom.

Waugh was more inclined to question than to issue manifestoes, literary or political. In the late 1920s, he allied himself with writers like Ronald Firbank, Wyndham Lewis, Ernest Hemingway, and Henry Green (pseudonym of his Oxford contemporary Henry Yorke) to advocate, in contrast to modernist stream of consciousness and other subjective approaches (including, ironically, first person narrators), objective methods in fiction, but he apparently did not formulate and certainly did not issue proclamations about the subject. Like most of his generation, he simply ignored politics, and though he commented on contemporary manners and mores in profitable journalism, he seemed to have no program, besides common sense, individuality, and reticence, for changing attitudes or behavior. He did not conceal his Catholicism—in fact, he published articles about his conversion and wrote a prize-winning biography of Edmund Campion, which he dedicated to Martin d'Arcy, S. J., the priest who received him into the Catholic church—but his fiction remained so free of reference to religion that many of his readers thought, and some still think, that he became a Catholic just before he wrote *Brideshead.*

His social and political views were no more clearly stated in the fiction he published through 1942. *Vile Bodies,* a novel about the Bright Young People and about the collapse of the Establishment run by the older generation, combined farce and pathos and gained him not only popular notoriety but also the friendly notice of the fashionable world. He began to visit the Lygons at Madresfield (where he wrote much of his novel *Black Mischief*); he met young politicians like Randolph Churchill (son of Winston); and, as the 1930s progressed, he alternated novels more or less comic and satiric in tone with increasingly sober pronouncements on literature, art, architecture (his taste, like Ryder's, tended towards the neoclassical), and politics in which he spent more time attacking the opposition than in defending the establishment among whose members he moved and with whom he was most comfortable. After the publication of *A Handful of Dust* (1934), which corresponds roughly to Charles Ryder's paintings in presenting reemergent barbarism triumphing over civilization, Waugh strove to find a method that would allow him to comment more fully and more directly on his times.

In 1939, when World War II began, he was writing, in the voice of John Plant, a mystery novelist, a story intended to reflect and to comment in more direct and complex fashion than in previous novels on his own generation, forced to deal uneasily with responsibility for wives, children, houses, and careers suitable to grownups. He abandoned the novel when he went on active service with the Royal Marines, explaining that "even if I were again to have the leisure and will to finish it, the work would be vain, for the world in which and for which it was designed, has ceased to exist" (*Work Suspended*, 7).

His motives for seeking active service as a junior officer at the age of thirty-six were partly patriotic—he was initially and even through 1942 an enthusiastic officer—and partly literary. Looking to "thirty years of novel-writing ahead of me," he concluded that "Nothing would be more likely than work in a government office to finish me as a writer; nothing more likely to stimulate me than a complete change of habit."[2] Yet the war did not bring him either military or immediate literary success. Except for *Put Out More Flags,* a novel about characters from earlier novels in something like his earlier manner which he wrote during the leisurely sea voyage from Egypt to England, he wrote no fiction and only twenty fugitive articles, reviews, and letters to the editor from 1940 through 1943.

By late 1943, relegated to noncombatant status, he was disillusioned with his military career, fairly sure that the Allies would defeat the German-Italian-Japanese Axis, gloomy about conditions in England, and apprehensive that political trends towards socialism would destroy the world he had known. As a writer, he worried that his talents were lying fallow and that, like vintage wine, some of his experience had to be used before it spoiled.

Less than a month after he expressed these views in his diary, he spent a late night drinking at White's, one of his London clubs, and then went on a mission of mercy to visit Hubert Duggan, who was obviously on his deathbed. Waugh returned several times, finally, over the objection of some of Duggan's relatives, bringing a priest to give Duggan absolution and what was at that time called extreme unction, the sacrament for the dying. Duggan thanked the priest after the first visit and crossed himself after the second, and Waugh noted that "we spent the day watching for a spark of gratitude for the love of God and saw the spark" (*Diaries*, 553).

Duggan's deathbed repentance had a catalytic effect on Waugh's imagination. Later he would ridicule the writers who, "averting themselves sickly from privations of war and apprehensions of the social consequences of the peace, were even then severally and secretly, unknown to one another . . . composing or preparing to compose books which would turn from the drab alleys of the thirties into the odorous gardens of a recent past transformed and illuminated by disordered memory and imagination."[3]

Even in caricaturing *Brideshead Revisited* Waugh drew, as he did in all of his writing, on his memories and his knowledge of the contemporary scene. *Brideshead* was more realistic in method and more explicitly concerned with the interaction of memory and social milieu (of which dates, names, and details are historically accurate) than his previous fiction. For that reason he may have felt it necessary to provide the reader with the disclaimer that appears in the "Author's Note."

That disclaimer needs some qualification. Though clearly based on Duggan's, Lord Marchmain's deathbed repentance was placed more dramatically, just before the beginning of the war, which perhaps grew out of and certainly altered the direction of the lives of the characters and, by implication, that of the society in which they lived in the decades between two world wars. But other characters and incidents were altered less. Waugh drew the arrest for public drunkenness in chapter 5 of book 1 from an episode involving him and his aristocratic codefendant Matthew Ponsonby in 1925. Anthony Blanche is based upon a blend of the characters and tastes of Brian Howard and Harold Acton. Lord Marchmain's family and exile abroad (though not the motive for his exile or the architecture of his country seat, Madresfield) have obvious origins in Lord Beauchamp and the Lygon family. Minor characters like Mr. Samgrass and Rex Mottram have been linked with Sir Maurice Bowra, a popular Oxford don with whom Waugh maintained a mutually derisive friendship for most of his life, and Brendan Bracken, Winston Churchill's wartime minister of information. Before turning to literature as a last resort Waugh wanted to be an artist; and, according to his brother Alec, his tone of voice toward people of whom he disapproved was identical to Charles Ryder's toward his wife in chapter 1 of part 2. Only once did Waugh reply publicly to the question "Are your characters drawn from life?" As far as his answer went, it was candid: "In the broadest sense, of course, they are. None except one or two negligible minor figures is a portrait; all the major characters are the result of numberless diverse observations fusing in the imagination into a single whole."[4]

The same response might be applied to the milieu of the book. In *Brideshead* Waugh did not attempt a comprehensive portrait of England between the wars, but he did draw upon public events as well as personal memories to give an imaginative portrait not of the world but of a world.

2

The Importance of the Work

Questions about the importance of any work of art derive from the critical tradition which holds that the function of literature is to delight and to teach, perhaps, put crudely, to lure the reader with aesthetic bait that conceals the moral hook. But critics tend to assume that in masterpieces of literature the distinction between beauty and doctrine all but disappears and the work and responses to it are seamless wholes.

We read literary works for a variety of reasons and have an even wider range of responses, many of them unconscious or at least imperfectly formulated, and as new readers come to a work that matures or simply grows older, the views about delight and instruction, or beauty and truth, tend to change. Evelyn Waugh himself, returning to the novel fifteen years after he wrote it, confessed that events had not justified the gloom of his social prophecies and recognized in the style of the work the effects of a nostalgia for physical and stylistic luxuries which, in revising, he tried to purge.

Waugh originally wrote for an audience that was enduring the rationing of food and clothing and, to some tastes, an even more severe aesthetic privation. Therefore, the elements of romance had a great deal to do with the original success of the novel in England. More startling—at least to Waugh, who predicted to his agent that not six Americans would understand the novel—was its reception in this country and among readers of all ages and classes. *Brideshead Revisited* is probably the only Book-of-the-Month Club selection to be studied in the Masterwork series, and when it was lovingly and lavishly produced as a television miniseries, it attained even wider popularity—all eleven episodes were broadcast throughout the English-speaking world in 1981–82. Those who read the very limited edition that Waugh sent as a Christmas present to a very few friends in 1944 no doubt experienced nostalgia. Americans and later English readers, for whom the novel is, in varying degrees of vagueness, "historical," experience a kind of wish fulfillment.

The attraction of the novel's superficial glamor must be admitted, and some critics, deploring it, can see nothing else in the novel. But there is more to recommend the novel even on the aesthetic plane. The characters are varied and interesting and not wholly unlike people someone with moderately broad experience is likely to meet. There are undoubtedly more Rex Mottrams and Samgrasses than Anthony Blanches, which, from a stylistic point, explains the impoverishment of political and academic discourse. Many readers have been drawn into the plot, perhaps because the internal rhythms consistently carry actors and audience from the mundane or hopeless to a point, however small, of rest and resolution. Considering plot in more conventional terms, Chaim Potok, an American Jewish novelist, has said that he became so involved in Lord Marchmain's deathbed scene that, like Charles Ryder, he hoped intensely for the sign—and on cooler reflection, decided that he wanted to practice the art that could transcend barriers of country, class, and religion.[5] On the technical level—style, arrangement of characters and incidents, and construction of the whole—the novel can be profitably studied as well as read for entertainment.

As for the question of the book's enduring value, of why it matters, both Charles Ryder and Evelyn Waugh would say, without rancor or shame, that, finally, it does not matter, that the divine goal of salvation is infinitely more important than any human conception of the process, however elegantly that conception might be embodied. Ryder's paintings in the garden room have been obliterated; there is no indication in the novel that he will ever practice his art again; the castle is being despoiled and the carefully planned and planted grounds will become a gunnery range.

Yet the art and the action matter—because art makes them matter. As in all pastoral elegy—John Milton's "Lycidas," Percy Bysshe Shelley's "Adonais," W. H. Auden's "In Memory of William Butler Yeats"—the speaker must find in an occasion for despair some element of hope. Unlike his predecessors in elegiac poetry, Waugh treats not the loss of any one beloved person but of a whole way of life. Some critics (see chapter 3) cannot see beyond the novel's love of the superficial glamour of that way of life and what they see as the snobbery in presenting and evaluating those who live it. But the novel deals on a deeper level not with great houses and their titled inhabitants but with the way in which human activity and experience, including aesthetic experience, including love, are not just momentary frictions or thrills but profound shapers of human destiny. Human works are not in themselves important, but they are not, in the religious or social sense, vain. To reject or ignore the human past, individual or collective, is to make oneself, like Rex Mottram, less than fully human.

Finally, although perhaps too obliquely for some readers, *Brideshead Revisited* is about what it means to be human rather than a tiny fragment of a human being. Individual characters may fail to become human (and, as usual in literature, are more interesting than those who succeed); Charles Ryder may fail as both character and narrator to become human. The point—on which believers in various schools of psychology, philosophy, and religion can agree—is that the process of becoming human cannot end in life nor, no matter what the consolation in the technical elegiac sense, should it be closed off in literature.

3

Critical Reception

Brideshead Revisited has always been more popular with readers than with critics—including the author himself when he reread the novel more than a decade after writing it. Only in recent years, as critics have become more detached from the political, social, and religious contexts that gave rise to the novel and that are reflected in it, have they begun to distinguish the art of the novel as a whole from contingent if not extraneous thematic considerations. And even now the tradition of critical disapproval and Waugh's defensive attitude toward the novel, at first implicit and then explicit, places the burden of proof on those who find it a complex and satisfying work of art.

The critical reception of *Brideshead* can be traced either historically or topically. The historical method presents the attitudes of reviewers at the time of publication and then shows the ways in which these attitudes help to shape those views voiced in longer critical works that consider the place of the novel in Waugh's work as a whole. The next stage in the process of evaluation takes place after publication of the Uniform Edition in 1960. More than two decades later, in 1981 and 1982, a new generation of critics evaluated the novel in light of the television version. Since the late 1950s, scholars had been trying to place the novel in the contexts of Waugh's development as a novelist and of the milieu in which he wrote, but logically, and to some extent chronologically, this is a further stage in a process that will last as long as people—not just publishing scholars or critics—read the novel.

The historical method shows that initially *Brideshead Revisited* received very high praise in the secular as well as the Catholic press. Critical opinion began to turn against the novel early in 1946, and the grounds on which negative criticisms were based have dominated discussion for more than four decades. Only gradually have scholars begun to see the architectonics of the novel as a whole and to counter some of the most damaging charges leveled by its detractors.

While a discussion of the progress of a work's reputation can tell us a great deal about the history of critical taste, it necessarily involves making distinctions among slight variations in critical opinion and therefore a good deal of repetition. More directly informative about the novel itself is the topical approach which, in the case of *Brideshead Revisited,* involves three major issues. First, and in a sense encompassing the other two, is the issue of the place of the novel in Waugh's development as a writer. Does *Brideshead* reveal a major shift in Waugh's themes and techniques? If so, is the change for better or for worse? If for worse, has he abused his talent or has he simply revealed limitations more easily concealed in less ambitious work? Involved in these questions are considerations of genre and mode, or what form and tone the novel has or should have. The second issue deals with the religious theme, asking whether it is a valid one for the period and for the novel genre, and, if so, whether Waugh has embodied the theme in a convincing manner. The third issue deals with the technique of the novel, all the way from the proportions of the novel (a structural consideration) to the language of individual scenes and even sentences, which involves style in the broadest sense. And since, in 1960, Waugh's revisions concentrated on style and structure, the history of the text (technically a separate matter involving physical evidence of the author's revisions as well as speculation about his intention) is directly relevant to this third issue and more tenuously related to the others.

Evelyn Waugh was the first to be aware of these issues, and it could be argued that he went out of his way to call attention to them in various published statements. When he began, in January 1944, to write what was then called "A Household of the Faith," he intended that *Brideshead* should represent a major shift in his themes and methods. Pleased that he had begun to acquire a style, he called the novel, with only a degree of levity, his "Magnum Opus" (*Diaries, 560*). To Lady Dorothy Lygon, a member of one family on whom the Flytes were loosely modeled, he wrote, "I am writing a very beautiful book, to bring tears, about very rich, beautiful, high born people who live in palaces and have no troubles except what they make themselves and those are mainly the demons sex and drink which after all are easy to bear as troubles go nowadays," and later he insisted that "it will go on being read for many years."[6]

By the time the novel was finally published in June 1945, he was aware that the general audience might be less happy than he was with his new theme and style. The novel's subtitle, "The Sacred and Profane Memories of Captain Charles Ryder," offered a fairly broad hint of the change, but he went further and included a "Warning" on the dust jacket flap of the English edition. In 1928, his publishers had asked him to warn readers that his first novel, *Decline and Fall*, "was meant to be funny." *Brideshead*, in which "the general theme is at once romantic and eschatological," was not. Rather, it was intended as

> an attempt to trace the workings of the Divine purpose in a pagan world, in the lives of an English Catholic family, half-paganized themselves, in the world of 1923–1939. The story will be uncongenial alike to those who look back on that pagan world with unalloyed affection, and to those who see it as transitory, insignificant, and, already, hopefully passed. Whom, then, can I hope to please? Perhaps those who have the leisure to read a book word by word for the interest of the writer's use of language; perhaps those who look to the future with black foreboding and need more solid comfort than rosy memories. For the latter, I have given my hero, and them, if they will allow me, a hope, not, indeed, that anything but disaster lies ahead, but that the human spirit, redeemed, can survive all disasters.[7]

It is clear from these remarks that Waugh knew that he had redefined and very probably limited his audience, that he was aware of the grounds on which this might happen, and that he was content with the prospect.

By the time he wrote the "Warning," he had already received Lady Pansy Lamb's view that the world of the 1920s was trivial and transitory. He withstood this view and the reactions, just after publication, of friends from his Oxford years who served as models for characters in the novel and who teased him about supposed autobiographical aspects of the story and reported devastating parodies of key scenes (*Letters*, 199 n. 2; *Diaries*, 626).

Partly because *Brideshead* was a Book-of-the-Month Club selection, the American edition was not published until January 1946. Popular success was a foregone conclusion, and some of the critics were equally enthusiastic. But Edmund Wilson, who in 1944 had hailed Waugh as "the only first-rate comic genius that has appeared in English since Bernard Shaw," mounted an assault on the novel that set the tone and established the major issues for the ensuing four decades of criticism. Wilson found the first half of the novel "invested with a poetry and staged with a dramatic effectiveness which seem to promise . . . the habitual reader of Waugh . . . that his favorite has been fledged as a first-rank straight novelist." But "when Waugh abandons his comic convention," the result is "disastrous" because "his deficiency in common sense" leads him into "romantic fantasy" of situation and "dispiriting clichés" of style, with the result that snobbery emerges "shameless and rampant" as "the only real religion" in a book that is apparently intended as "a Catholic tract."[8]

In a letter to his agent, Waugh rejoiced that "we have shaken off Edmund Wilson at last" (*Letters*, 218). After all, less than a month into writing the novel Waugh had predicted that "not six Americans will understand it" (*Letters*, 177). "Fan-Fare," Waugh's watch-my-lips response to his American readers, represented little change in this attitude. Waugh refuted charges that he used clichés by asserting that "to be oversensitive about clichés is like being oversensitive about table manners. It comes from keeping second-rate company. Professional reviewers . . . get an unhealthy craving for arresting phrases." Charges of snobbery he rejected on the grounds that "Class consciousness, particularly in England, has been so much inflamed nowadays that to mention a nobleman is like mentioning a prostitute sixty years ago. The new prudes say, 'No doubt such people do exist but we would sooner not hear about them.' I reserve the right to deal with the kind of people I know best" (*Essays*, 394). But the biggest sales of his career and the flood of praise from America had shaken his faith in the novel, and to Lady Mary Lygon he ruefully confessed that "I thought it in good taste before and now it can't be" (*Letters*, 223).

By this time, the major topics of critical discussion of *Brideshead* had been established, and for some thirty years they were developed in much the same way. Some critics used the early comic novels to belabor the supposed deficiencies of *Brideshead*. As Marston LaFrance put it, "The comic sections of this novel . . . have a spontaneous life and freshness which is lacking in other parts of the novel. The best of *Brideshead Revisited* belongs with the earlier tradition; left with the reader are passages of empty rhetoric and a feeling that an attempt to force a serious frame upon an unconscious use of the comic tradition has not been entirely successful."[9] Others used *Brideshead* as evidence that the early novels had serious deficiencies. D. S. Savage has argued this point most forcefully: "Ironic detachment from the futile whirligig of human affairs is hardly an adequate or promising attitude for a serious writer, even for a serious comic writer, for the richest humour is bred from fullness and not paucity of life. . . . A consideration of his two 'serious' novels leads only to a substantiation of this discovery of his fundamental and inescapable immaturity. . . . [They] succeed in supplementing each other in their documentation of his impotence as a serious writer."[10]

Implied in this particular judgment is a view that only specifically human, or humanist, material could or should be presented in fiction. Savage thinks that the novel should have been about Charles Ryder's marriage to Celia, but he is not alone in ignoring the religious theme. Other secular critics recognized, and deplored, the introduction or intrusion of religion into a novel of contemporary life. Anglicans like

Rose Macaulay lamented the narrow sectarianism that identified religion with Roman Catholicism. Frank Kermode began an article in a secular journal by referring to "Papists," a traditional English slur word for Catholics that promised very little objectivity in the discussion of Waugh's historical and religious intransigence that followed. Even Irish Catholics like Conor Cruise O'Brien (writing in 1947 under the pseudonym Donat O'Donnell) and Sean O'Faolain thought that Waugh had so mixed religion and secular concerns, including English romanticism and social snobbery, that although "the theme . . . is universally valid," "the treatment is not."[11]

Distaste for or disquiet about the religious theme accounts for some of the criticism of the novel's structure. Many critics have felt that book 2, which returns or brings the major characters to the Catholic church, is disproportionately brief or, less commonly, that the apparently nonreligious chapters set in Oxford are disproportionately long; and some argue that the lack of development in book 2 helps to account for the almost universal judgment (a notable exception is a Russian critic) that Julia is a thoroughly unconvincing character.[12]

Julia is a crucial figure because much of the criticism of the novel's style focused on the presentation of Charles Ryder's love affair with her. Henry Reed thought those scenes like "a gaudy novelette." Marston LaFrance objected to the "self-consciously poetic padding" in these and other passages, and David Lodge argued that "The extended images . . . though elaborated with elegance and beauty, seem drawn from literary stereotypes rather than experience."[13]

Some of these judgements were made after Waugh's death in 1966, but they represent critical views that Waugh had already acknowledged. With some of them he came to agree. Writing to Graham Greene, he "was appalled. I can find many excuses . . . but [the style] won't do for peace-time" (*Letters*, 322). Having gone through the novel word by word in preparing the 1960 Uniform Edition, he achieved a somewhat more balanced and objective tone in discussing the novel which according to Waugh, "lost me such esteem as I once enjoyed among my contemporaries." Although he admitted that "Its theme—the operation of divine grace on a group of diverse but closely connected characters—was perhaps presumptuously large," he refused to apologize for it. The embodiment of that theme was another matter, and he traced the "glaring defects" to the circumstances of writing in "the period of soya beans and Basic English," so that "the book is infused with a kind of gluttony, for food and wine, for the splendours of the recent past, and for rhetorical and ornamental language, which now with a full stomach I find distasteful." Yet "the grosser passages . . . are an essential part of the book," which he had come to regard "as a souvenir of the Second War rather than of the twenties or of the thirties, with which it ostensibly deals" (*Brideshead*, 1960, 10). And he either acknowledged criticisms of the novel's structure or decided that the principle of division he had used in manuscript had merit, for he divided the two books of all previously published editions into three by making the final three chapters of book 1 into book 2, "Brideshead Deserted," in an attempt to bridge or conceal the ten-year gap in time and character development between "Et in Arcadia Ego" and "A Twitch upon the Thread."

In view of Waugh's concessions about the novel, it might seem that there was little left to say in its defense. Still, even the most severe critics of the novel have found virtues in some of the characters, scenes, and even whole sections. Furthermore, literary criticism often seems to develop less by answering old questions than by raising new ones or by giving old ones a new twist in order to see a work in a new way.

One major new area of discussion has dealt with the genre of *Brideshead*. Hostile critics had seen it as a sort of upscale Harlequin Romance, with Charles Ryder as the outsider trying to marry up and in. Others regarded it as an uneasy and unsuccessful mishmash of satire and romance. More recent critics have looked not at the tone but at the narrator and have argued that *Brideshead* is a "novel of conversion" (Joseph Hynes), or a bildungsroman (John Edward Hardy and Thomas Prufer), or the subgenre of that subgenre, the künstlerroman (artist-novel) (Jeffrey Heath). This is not just an exercise in juggling labels but an attempt to discover exactly who, and therefore what, the novel is about and from that vantage point to decide what structural and stylistic choices are appropriate to this particular embodiment of the genre.[14]

By focusing on Ryder, these critics ignore Waugh's statement in the 1945 "Warning" that the novel was about the Flyte family. Other critics, including John Coleman in 1960 and Edward Pearce in 1982, ignored another statement of intention. If they read the "Author's Note," which explicitly states "I am not I; thou art not he or she; they are not they," they seemed to assume that it merely denied autobiographical sources of character and incident. In any case, they regarded Ryder's opinions and sympathies as identical with Waugh's, attributing to the author the jejune and snobbish statements of the narrator. Jeffrey Heath exaggerates only a little in holding "that most adverse criticism really originates in a distaste for Charles Ryder."[15]

The real critical question for this or any novel written in first person is the degree of distance—intellectual, moral, social, and in this case religious—not only between the novelist and his creation but also between the "I" as narrator and the "I" as actor. In the first American book-length study of Waugh, James Carens simply assumed that Charles Ryder's views are Waugh's. In the first book-length study, Frederick J. Stopp was not sure that their views were distinct. But in the most thorough analysis of point of view in Waugh's novels, William J. Cook argues that there are in fact three "Charles Ryders": the "now-I" of the prologue and epilogue, the "then-I" or actor in the events of the past, and an "intermediate-I" who is never dramatically presented but whose voice serves as a surrogate omniscient voice in the body of the novel.[16]

Other critics are less directly concerned with point of view and with narrative technique, but they do examine Charles as a character, not so much for what he says but for why he says it, which has an important bearing upon his reliability as narrator. Ruth Wilson traces to his "early emotional deprivation" the fact that "in his human relationships he can never quite commit himself" and that only for moments can he sustain his artistic passion. Thomas Prufer argues that though Charles tells the story of the Flytes, "Without them he is unformed, pale, empty, 'dim.' " This point is important both technically and thematically: "For artistic reasons Waugh makes Charles dim because Charles is the colorless eye which sees all colors; but for theological reasons Waugh makes Charles dim because the gain of the life of grace does not substitute for nature in nature's own terms and on nature's own terms."[17]

Other critics, responding specifically to the television version as well as the novel, show that one can respond intelligently to *Brideshead* without employing the technical vocabulary of literary criticism. For example, Lawrence O'Toole implicitly refutes the criticism that book 1 is too long not, like James Carens, by counting pages, but by responding to the way in which the story "has so ardently impressed the imagery of Arcadia upon the viewer that the feeling of being let down is so powerful, because it is so necessary. . . . [T]he length and leisure are important in showing the slow triumph of shadow over the sunlit promise of the beginning."[18]

Few responses to this or any other work are entirely wrong, though some combine myopia with tunnel vision. If some of the recent ways of looking at the novel seem superior to others, it is not because they canonize the novel—even the most favorable critics express some reservations—or even because they exhibit a deeper understanding of the text or reassure us about our own tastes. But they do find in the text a richness and complexity previously undiscovered because they are willing to see the work in a fresh, thoughtful, and ultimately generous manner.

A READING

4

Backgrounds Sacred and Profane

Students in my introduction to fiction class said they enjoyed *Brides-head Revisited* because, for a change, they were reading about normal people doing normal things. Because these "normal things" involve crisis and displacement from an historical point of view; extreme class consciousness from a social point of view; pride, covetousness, lust, anger, gluttony, envy, and sloth from the religious point of view; and a very complex theory about the ascent from earthly love to divine love, one must assume either that my students have grown up in a very interesting world or they have been reading and viewing works that present even more unusual situations.

The students' response was a tribute to Waugh's skill, because very few of us came from titled families or went to Oxford or have gotten drunk in settings this elegant or were raised as Catholics or Neo-Platonists. Like all writers, Waugh was faced with the problem of presenting new information so that his readers would not only find it comprehensible but would accept it as a normal part of the fictional world that they chose to enter and which, if bored or confused or in any way dissatisfied, they could leave at will. The first person narrator was his most important way of dealing with this problem, and, as chapter 3 indicated and as chapter 6 will discuss in more detail, the reader's response to Charles Ryder will dictate the response to and evaluation of the novel.

Although finally readers must resist the temptation to divide form and content, they can understand the novel more clearly if they have a sense of the materials upon which Waugh's imagination worked before I turn, in subsequent chapters, to the workings of that imagination. Moreover, although the Catholic Church and the English class system still exist, many contemporary readers are not familiar with the asumptions that lie behind them, and in some cases the customs described in the novel are no longer current. Thus the material that follows is presented as historical even when the past tense is not always strictly accurate and is based upon Waugh's personal response to events, doctrines, and assumptions that he expected readers to understand if not share.

For example, Waugh's view of World War II was from the beginning very different from that of most Englishmen. While he was less naive than Guy Crouchback in *Sword of Honour,* who regarded the war as a crusade and rejoiced that the alliance between Russia and Germany put the forces of evil on one side, Waugh did see the conflict less in strategic than in moral terms. England's subsequent alliance with Russia disappointed him as a Catholic while it may have heartened him as a soldier. But in 1943, when it seemed probable that the Allies would defeat the German-Italian-Japanese Axis, and still more strongly in 1944, when preparations to invade Normandy were being made without any role for him, he found little to cheer him in his personal military career. He had been stationed in a camp much like that described in the prologue, and though his war experiences were somewhat more exciting than those of Charles Ryder, he had been separated from old friends and social equals and superiors and relegated to the dullest kind of soldiering. And like all Englishmen, he had endured four years of rationing and less tangible limitations. Day-to-day morale was so low that in writing *1984* George Orwell did not have to imagine the personal circumstances of Winston Smith—he had lived through them in London during the last years of the war. As

Waugh said in the preface to the 1960 edition of *Brideshead*, "It was a period of present privation and threatening disaster—the period of soya beans and Basic English" (1960 *Brideshead*, 9).

Furthermore, though it seemed clear that the Allies were going to win the war, it was far from clear what the victory would mean for the kind of life Waugh had known. The ravages of war would have to be repaired—not only the public effects of bombs but also the personal effects, such as the convent of nuns renting his country home, Piers Court. In addition, there had been a good deal of propaganda about reordering the entire economic, educational, and social fabric of English law and life and some questioning of the patriotism of the upper classes. The prospect of these changes accounts for the bitterness with which Ryder contemplates a future designed for Hooper where "the ancestral seats which were our chief national artistic achievement were doomed to decay and spoliation like the monasteries in the sixteenth century" (preface, *Brideshead*, 1960, 10). The Labour Party's attempt to embody these changes in the Welfare State led Waugh to think, in 1947, about emigrating to Ireland. By 1960, he realized that his pessimism was excessive, that "The advance of Hooper has been held up at several points," and thus he came to regard *Brideshead* not as prophecy but "as a souvenir of the Second War."

Waugh realized that not everyone, including some of his best friends, would agree with his diagnosis of the past or his predictions for the future. In fact, some of his best friends were very aristocratic socialists. But he could assume that all of his English readers would be familiar with the nuances of the English class system. In the prediction that "not six Americans will understand" the novel (*Letters*, 177), he was perhaps thinking of the nuances of social and educational hierarchies of which Americans would be all but invincibly ignorant.

While the cast of characters in *Brideshead Revisited* stretches all the way from royalty, in the Duke of Clarence's brief appearance at Ryder's exhibition, to members of the "other ranks" in the army, the major line of social demarcation falls somewhat below Charles Ryder and above his commanding officer. Waugh and his friend Nancy Mitford traded lines in essays about class published as *Noblesse Oblige*,[19] in which the terms "U" and "Non-U," or Upper and Non-Upper, were defined and applied to distinctions in language, manners, and taste. Everyone who went to a public school (in England these are ancient and elitist; American prep schools are rather pale imitations) or Oxford or Cambridge universities was either U to start with or had the potential to become U. Scholarships were available for bright students from lower (though not the lowest) income brackets, but the social expectations and the general atmosphere were not established with them in mind. As the novel strongly implies, Oxford prepared its students not so much for careers as for life in a clearly defined society. For one thing, examinations were fewer and more widely spaced, though the final examinations, which covered three years' work, were far more serious than anything encountered by American undergraduates. In the 1920s (and even today) a far smaller percentage of English than American students went to universities. Moreover, while other universities existed, Oxford and Cambridge so far outstripped them in prestige and endowment that it was as if America had Harvard and Yale at the top and then a number of vocational schools, and no gradations between.

It was possible to remain U without having very much money, but it was not possible, as Rex Mottram's career illustrates, to become U merely by amassing money or even power. Instead, as the novel implies, it is Non-U to worry or even to know very much about one's income or social status. It was important to carry on tradition, as Bridey conscientiously and ineptly tries to do, but it is not entirely clear, in the terms established in the novel, how or even why the carrying on will be done. U people, used to servants, were supposed to be "good" with them. Sebastian was not unusual in having a nanny—Waugh, from a class slightly below Ryder's, had one—or in being attached to her, though his attachment is abnormal and unhealthy. This life-style took money, of course. The Flytes are obviously very rich, but Charles Ryder's father is far from poor—though, like the Flytes, he is spending inherited capital rather than living off the income from capital.

Far more important in determining aristocratic status in the world of *Brideshead* is background: family, class, education. Lady Marchmain finds Rex unsuitable as a prospective son-in-law because he is an outsider, which means that no one knows anything about him or about his potential as breeding stock; because his manners, habits, and values are not those of her class; and last of all, because he is not a Catholic. Critics have complained that the dinner in Paris reveals that Charles, and Waugh, is a hopeless snob about food and wine, but the scene indicates that Rex is even more snobbish and immeasurably more ignorant. On the other hand, Mulcaster has background and money, but he is far more loutish than Hooper.

Of course, there were distinctions among peers (from bottom to top, barons, earls, viscounts, marquesses, dukes, royal dukes, princes, queen/king) and the commoners and the descendants of peers and commoners. People at Oxford, and elsewhere, considered being the son of a wealthy and powerful peer better than descending from a poor and weak commoner—or even a richer and more powerful commoner. Rex is aware of this when he plans to marry Julia, and if they had had children, he would have been quite content to have them universally described as the descendants of the Marquess of Marchmain rather than the direct offspring of a member of Parliament or a cabinet officer or whatever rank, even a peerage, an honor that he might attain on his own. And, like Celia, Julia is called "Lady" in formal address no matter whom she marries or divorces.

Non-U people were not necessarily lower class, but they were very definitely not the right sort. Ryder has difficulty in dealing with Hooper and with his commanding officer not just because they are incompetent but because they have a different vocabulary and scale of values because of their (quite different) social and educational backgrounds. On the other hand, while he dislikes Mr. Samgrass and Anthony Blanche, they speak a dialect intelligible to him. Servants, like Wilcox the butler and Nanny, were definitely not U but they were not exactly Non-U. Ryder may not speak the language of Nanny Hawkins, but the two of them share a framework of social references and values that Ryder and Hooper cannot share.

Class and taste are taken so much for granted in the novel that Waugh did not always feel the need to give overt explanations of their workings. But he faced more complex problems in dealing with religion not only because he was writing for nonbelievers as well as Catholics, but also because he wanted his readers to sympathize with his theme as well as understand his characters. The oddest thing about my students' response to the novel is that they did not object to situations in which religious motives and practice drive the plot, notably Lord Marchmain's deathbed repentance and its effects, which have mortally offended secular critics. These critics were paying attention: Waugh told his agent that the novel was "steeped in theology" (*Letters*, 185), had an expert check the manuscript for accuracy,[20] and concluded that very few readers would understand the theological implications. This was not just fussiness: he insisted both in the "Warning" in the first English edition and in later comments that he saw religion as the basis not only of the plot but of the conception of character presented "fully, which, to me, means only one thing, man in his relation to God" (*Essays*, 302).

Just as Waugh insisted that *Brideshead* was not like secular novels, he would have insisted, like Sebastian, that Catholics were not like other people, and before the second Vatican Council ended in 1965, they were less like other people than they have since become. In England, they had been much less like other people than elsewhere because they had been excluded, systematically and legally, from various kinds of political and social power from the mid-sixteenth century until 1829, only four years before the abolition of slavery in all British possessions. A hundred years earlier, Bridey and Sebastian could not have gone to Oxford. Even now, a member of the Royal Family who marries a Roman Catholic loses all rights to succeed to the throne, a rule of which Julia is acutely aware when she considers the possibilities of marriage. Of course, very few Catholics in England were concerned with this kind of problem. Many were, like Father Mackay in chapter 5 of book 2, descended from Irish immigrants and socially of no consequence. Only a few aristocratic families had, like Lady Marchmain's, remained Catholic since the disruptions of the sixteenth century. In fact, the term "Roman Catholic" was politically charged; some Anglicans insisted on the distinction between "English" and

"Roman" Catholic, while "real" ("Roman") Catholics rejected any geographical modifier as a contradiction in terms, because "catholic" is by definition without limit. Anyone who thinks these distinctions meaningless has not been following the news from Belfast, where the issues, though not identical, are similar.

Catholics were also different from other people, including other Christians, in a spiritual sense. (I am, as I said earlier, adopting the viewpoint and tense of a specific historical period.) One became Catholic by a valid baptism. (Catholics recognized that baptism in other denominations could be valid, but converts received "conditional baptism" in case the first one didn't take.) Baptism removed the stain of original sin (inherited from Adam) and rendered the soul capable of receiving God's grace, without which salvation (Heaven) could not be attained and damnation (Hell) could not be avoided. Like confirmation and holy orders, baptism was one of three of the seven sacraments (penance, holy Eucharist, matrimony, and extreme unction were the others) that could only be received once and that left an indelible spiritual mark upon the soul. This meant that once you became a Catholic, you always remained a Catholic. You could not resign. You could be excommunicated (that is, like Julia after her marriage to Rex, you could not receive the Body and Blood of Christ in communion as the apostles had at the Last Supper), but you could not be stricken from the invisible rolls no matter what sins you committed or how strongly you tried to deny your faith. Indelible meant just that. And if you did not have that mark, you were not a member of the Mystical Body of Christ, which encompassed the church triumphant (souls in Heaven, who could intercede for the other two groups), the church suffering (souls in purgatory expiating temporal punishment due to sin, as opposed to eternal punishment being suffered in hell), and the church militant (souls still on earth who could offer good works for those in purgatory or for one another). There were some loopholes, but except for Julia's somewhat loose interpretation of invincible ignorance (which in fact meant not having had the opportunity to become a Catholic, not, as she thinks, in not being born and raised in a Catholic family) they do not figure in the novel.

The point is that Waugh and all Catholics believed that membership in the church was the surest way to salvation, and this accounts for Cordelia's pleasure in amassing African namesakes, for Lady Marchmain's desire to convert Charles, and for Charles's implied satisfaction at the end that "a surprising lot" (346) of soldiers use the chapel. From the outside, the desire to convert others may have looked imperialistic; from the inside, it was seen as an act of charity.

Sin was a more complex matter in *Brideshead*. In extreme views, including the novels of Waugh's friend Graham Greene, it sometimes seemed that you had to be a Catholic to be able to commit sin as distinguished from doing wrong. This distinction depends upon the traditional Christian theology that held that evil as such does not exist (thus avoiding Manichean views that would give Satan equal status with God). Instead, evil was a negation or denial—often described as the choice of a lesser over a greater good. Someone who did not know the greatest good—God—could not reject it for something less. For example, human love is good, but choosing it over the love of God, as Julia does in marrying Rex and in living with Charles and is tempted to do again by marrying Charles, is sinful. But Celia and Rex, though they commit adultery, are not, in the terms of the novel, presented as sinners. Bridey is, as always, quite orthodox in describing wine as a possible good and in finding consolation in belief that, as an alcoholic, Sebastian is not choosing to misuse one of God's gifts and to place it above his duty to know, love, and serve God and to be happy with Him in Heaven.

Good was defined as conformity with the will of God, but for practical purposes this meant following not only the Ten Commandments but also the laws of the church, summarized in the commandments of the church and elaborated in a very complex code of canon law. These rules have little direct bearing for the characters in *Brideshead*—except for the laws governing marriage. The major points of Catholic marriage law and custom prevailing during the period covered by the novel are explained to the bewildered Rex Mottram: Catholics were supposed to marry other Catholics. Mixed marriages (of religion, not race, as Rex thinks and as Lady Marchmain suggests) were grudgingly tolerated, but the non-Catholic partner was obliged to receive instruction in the faith, was made to promise that all children would be brought up as Catholics, and was reminded of the unsuitability of the whole process by going through an abbreviated marriage ceremony, which, if held in a church at all, took place outside the altar rail that divided the sanctuary (by definition the holiest part of the church) from less sacred space.

This body of canon law and custom is crucial to the action of the novel. Rex cannot marry Julia in any kind of Catholic ceremony because he has already been married, presumably in a valid ceremony. The characters raise and then dismiss the possibility of an annulment, which is very different from divorce. A divorce put an end to a civil contract; an annulment declared that a valid marriage never existed, was null and void. Annulments could be secured—Waugh was granted one in 1936 on the grounds that neither party to his marriage to Evelyn Gardner regarded the ceremony as religious or binding—but the process was too long and complex for Waugh's characters to contemplate or his plot to bear. Thus, while Julia's marriage to Rex is civilly valid, under church law it did not exist, and therefore (as Bridey notes) Julia is as guilty of committing sin by sleeping with Rex as she is by sleeping with Charles, no matter what legal steps are taken.

In fact, under church law, Julia has never been married and could therefore licitly marry anyone whom canon law did not specifically exclude. The novel, perhaps deliberately, does not clarify Charles's status. Presumably, given Lady Celia's and his social status, he was married in an Anglican ceremony, recognized by the Catholic church as valid for Anglicans. It seems unlikely that either partner regarded the ceremony as religious or binding, but the issue of Charles's seeking an annulment is never raised. Leaving aside the practical considerations of presenting a case in a Vatican about to be surrounded by enemy territory in World War II, Julia apparently refuses to marry Charles not merely because she cannot do so validly, but because she renounces marriage to him under any circumstances.

In a long memorandum of 1946 about a proposed film version of the novel, Waugh accepted the necessity for adaptation, but he insisted that "there must be an impediment to the marriage of Julia and Charles" because "I regard it as essential that after having had a life of sin Julia should not be immediately rewarded with conventional happiness. She has a great debt to pay and we are left with her paying it." Waugh explictly rejected "a banal Hollywood ending,"[21] and in fact he made it quite clear on a number of occasions and in a number of ways that the novel was not about the romantic fate of Charles Ryder but about the deathbed repentance of Lord Marchmain. Who slept with whom was interesting in fiction and in life (Waugh loved gossip), but it is not necessarily the most important event in a person's spiritual life. Some critics, including his Oxford contemporary and lifelong friend Henry Yorke, objected that Waugh fixed the plot to make the deathbed scene climactic, and some objected as much to the splendor of the surroundings as the slenderness of the sign that the dying man makes.[22] As Waugh and Julia recognize, however, one must not only repent of one's sins but also do penance for them. It may seem unfair that Julia will have a longer period of expiation on earth than her father because she repented sooner, but Lord Marchmain will presumably expiate his sins in purgatory. In any case, in the spiritual, external realm, quality is, literally, infinitely more important than quantity.

The theological reasoning behind the distinction between quantity and quality was quite traditional, and, in fact, becomes a major thematic issue in Waugh's *The End of the Battle*. If God was infinitely good, then, because man was not, only through His grace could man attain unity with Him. God desired the salvation of the sinner—a doctrine implied in the title of book 2, "A Twitch upon the Thread"— and offered grace until the moment of death. Grace could be either accepted or rejected until that moment. If accepted, the soul went to heaven to enjoy the beatific vision and various lesser pleasures for all eternity. If refused, the soul went to hell for an eternity of torments spelled out most vividly in modern literature in the hell sermon of James Joyce's *A Portrait of the Artist as a Young Man*.[23]

Yet Waugh makes clear from the subtitle—"The Sacred and Profane Memories of Captain Charles Ryder"—that linking spiritual and secular values is crucial to the novel. After all, Waugh presented his characters not merely in the spiritual world but in the social world, dwelling, however deplorably, in the city of man more firmly or at least more obviously than in the City of God. A theological problem presents itself: if God is infinite and man limited, how can anything that is part of a fallen world, including sex, art, wine, and wealth, be acceptable to God? In terms of the novel, how can Charles Ryder regard his past as good yet willingly relinquish the people, talents, and pleasures that constituted his past? One answer to this question relies on the discussion of good and evil presented earlier. Since no thing or action can be evil, then anything that exists must contain some good, however low on the scale. But if there are gradations of good, then humans can proceed through greater knowledge, or be led by God's grace, from one step to the next, from the lowest to the highest.

This ladder of ascent, adapted from pre-Christian Neo-Platonic philosophy, underlies Ryder's belief "that to know and love one other human being is the root of all wisdom" (45) and provides the key not only to the incidents in the novel but also to their meaning. Charles's love of Sebastian enables him to perceive natural and artistic beauty in new ways and gives him access to a new kind of emotional life. As Cara explains, this love is good—but it is primarily a preparation for a better kind of love, by which she means marriage. Charles implicitly agrees with this idea when he tells Julia that Sebastian was "the forerunner," an anticipation of and preparation for Charles's love for Julia. Later Julia offers the corollary that "perhaps I am only a forerunner too," and Charles plays with the idea that "all our loves are merely hints and symbols . . . perhaps you and I are types and this sadness which some-times falls between us springs from disappointment in our search, each straining through and beyond the other, snatching a glimpse now and then of the shadow which turns the corner always a pace or two ahead of us" (303). This theory, which the character accepts provisionally but which the narrator and the novel deny, implies that love is divisible and that one lover must give way to a successor, more or less infinitely. This kind of love is essentially egocentric.

The novel provides an alternative and an end to the search for love if not to the process of learning to love. If there are good and better loves, then the paradigm demands a best—and that is the love of God, defined in Christian theology as a complete and selfless union. Moreover, in this pattern earlier and less perfect loves need not be abandoned because they are subsumed into and completed by the perfect love, or charity. Because Ryder comes to believe in God, he can accept Julia's decision not to marry him and understand her role in bringing him into the Catholic church and therefore a step closer to the love of God. As the prologue indicates, he is very far from being a saint. But as the epilogue demonstrates, the recovery of the link with his past and the practice of his new religion bring him an access of charity towards the people in his past, towards the army, and even towards Hooper, whose second "Rightyoh" he lets pass unreprimanded.

Waugh's experience and analysis of social and religious life in England provided the impulse from which Waugh wrote and the goal towards which he worked. The chapters that follow discuss the means—structure, style, and other elements of narrative technique—by which he embodied his vision.

5

Shaping Experience
in *Brideshead Revisited*

Some beginning readers seem to think that writers just sit down, seized by inspiration and oblivious to technical questions, and begin writing. Other readers, more experienced or cynical, believe that a writer works from a highly elaborate and sometimes original preconceived pattern. Like most novelists, Evelyn Waugh did both, sometimes alternately, sometimes at once. Like others, he discovered his plot and his theme as he thought, wrote, and reconsidered; using methods that he had practiced and that reflected his individual way of perceiving and organizing experience, modifying a character or adding a situation to bring together idea and story into a whole that was neither sermon nor entertainment but a work of art. All novelists (in fact, all writers and perhaps all human beings) go through something like this process, though some do it so rapidly in their minds that it is imperceptible even to themselves, and others leave no written record of it. Waugh was acutely aware of the process, and he left a large body of evidence by which it can be traced.

Judging from our own experience and from what we can learn of the practice of others, we know that we do not just sit down and write. First we decide to write something of a certain kind or for a certain purpose, and whether we are making out a grocery list or writing a letter, our initial decision involves a number of secondary decisions about subject matter, choice of language, and even the arrangement of the material. These initial choices are called genres, literary types or kinds. By formulating them, both writers and readers are able to decide what sort of work they are dealing with. From the theorist's point of view, genre is a complex matter involving matters of tone, style, structure, form, and narrative tradition. The idea of genre may sound deterministic, or at least prescriptive, and in some periods it was used in this way, yet a genre can be used well or badly.

In fact, everyone uses the concept of genre if not the term. For example, we can confidently predict that movies starring Sylvester Stallone or Chuck Norris will have a lot of action and body oil and very little self-reflection and that movies starring Charles Bronson or Clint Eastwood will resemble those with Stallone and Norris in some respects and each other in still other ways. And we also realize that Eastwood in particular sometimes makes different kinds of movies and that they will have different kinds of plot and characterization and even visual style.

Waugh did not define genres, but he obviously used them. *Decline and Fall* uses the devices of circular structure, rapid movement, and resurrecting characters who had apparently been killed off that Voltaire used in *Candide* more than a century and a half earlier. Waugh may not have thought of either book as an apologue or Menippean satire, but he obviously understood the features that critics assign to these types.

Just as *Bronco Billy* falls into a genre different from that of the Dirty Harry movies, so *Brideshead Revisited* was written in a genre very different from *Decline and Fall* and the other early novels. Waugh reflected as he wrote *Brideshead* that it might be "the first of my novels rather than the last" (*Diaries,* 566). Though he never used the term bildungsroman to describe *Brideshead,* the novel has many features of the novel of development, which typically presents the various stages by which a young person comes to maturity. When that person is an artist and the stages show the sources and development of the character's technique and vision, the genre is called a künstlerroman, or artist-novel. George Moore's *Confessions of a Young Man* is a classic example of this type; less pure but better known is James Joyce's *A Portrait of the Artist as a Young Man.*

At least one very perceptive critic, bothered by generic considerations that he does not quite define, has criticized *Brideshead Revisited* because it does not focus consistently enough on Charles Ryder's development as a painter and in fact does not so much as mention art in the epilogue.[24] Waugh obviously used elements of the künstlerroman, but he did not feel bound by that genre in creating a work that had its own structure and form.

At this point it may be useful to consider abstract literary theory because it has very concrete embodiment in the shape of the novel. Structure is not a difficult concept. Biologists, sociologists, MBAs, and literary critics would agree in general that structure has to do with the relationship of parts to a whole and parts of that whole to one another. And the least experienced reader can discover the external structure of a printed literary work: white spaces and often numbers divide major parts like stanzas and cantos in poetry; acts and scenes in drama; chapters and other divisions in fiction.

Form is much more difficult to define or describe. For example, the much abridged *Random House Dictionary* lists twenty definitions of the noun and nine of the verb, but there are only four definitions of structure as a noun and one as a verb. Form and structure are not quite the same, but they are not entirely different, and sometimes they are used interchangeably. Most people, including critics, would admit that form is a more fluid and dynamic concept than structure. It describes an internal unity that emerges from the experience of the whole rather than an external pattern imposed from the beginning.

Whatever terms are used, it is clear that both writers and readers are aware of the distinction between inner and outer modes of coherence and of the importance of making them support each other. For example, the Italian sonnet has fourteen lines rhyming *a b b a a b b a* in the first eight lines and *c d e c d e* or some variant in the last six. A poet who chooses this structure may either construct sentences that correspond to the stanza divisions or arrange them to work against the external structure. The poet may use the change in rhyme after eight lines to make a shift from one idea or emotion to another—for example, from presenting a situation to analyzing it. But however the parts are arranged, they respond in various ways to the external structure. Structure does not exist except in specific works. There is no such thing as "the Italian sonnet" (or "the epic poem" or "the pastoral elegy"); there are a number of sonnets in the Italian form by John Milton, William Wordsworth, William Butler Yeats, and a host of other poets. And the same holds true for any traditional literary genre for which structures have been defined.

Of course, if a poet sets out to write a sonnet, then that initial choice establishes definite technical limits and possibilities—and, at least in the sixteenth century, the subject matter, love. But if someone sets out to write a novel, the consequences are much less circumscribed. The whole point about the novel (which came to prominence during the eighteenth century, a period fascinated by roles and definitions) was that, by definition, it was "new." Various critics have tried to establish rules for the novel or at least to define various subgenres, but general opinion seems to define a novel as any book not represented as true and thick enough to stand on end. One difficulty is that, as examination of any five novels chosen at random will show, there is no agreement on an external structure for the novel. All of them can be divided into parts by typographical devices; most have chapters; some have books; some, like *Brideshead Revisited,* have all of these principles of division. But there are no rules about how many books or chapters are necessary in a novel; even critics do not bother to argue about this issue as they have, argued for instance, about whether a tragedy should have three, four, or five acts, and in which situations.

The novel does have to have a story with a beginning, middle, and end. Like poets who rebelled against the rules for sonnet length, rhyme scheme, and subject matter—George Meredith wrote sonnets sixteen lines long; Gerard Manley Hopkins shrank and expanded them according to very complex theories; John Milton used them for political commentary—novelists have worked against these loose constraints.

Some have emphasized motive over action; some have introduced multiple plots or multiple and mutually exclusive endings; some have played with their readers' expectations about plot, character, setting, and theme. The most common practice, at least since storytellers learned the value of a story within a story (as in *The Odyssey*) and certainly since the time of Henry James (d. 1916), was arranging the incidents not in their strict chronological order but according to some other principle. Waugh, seldom revolutionary, chose one of the oldest variations: establishing a situation in which a narrator moves into the past to tell a story and then returns to the present.

Yet, while this was a departure for him—his only previous use of a first person narrator had been in *Work Suspended,* abandoned when he entered military service—he also adapted to suit his new purpose principles of organization he had used in earlier novels and which he would use until the end of his career. From his first novel, *Decline and Fall* (1928), through *Put Out More Flags* (1942), the one preceding *Brideshead,* to *The End of the Battle* (1961), his last, he characteristically divided his novels into large blocks, calling them parts or books, and subdividing them into chapters and sometimes into even smaller units. One obvious reason for doing so was to emphasize parallel and contrasting events, as in the repetition of "The Passing of a Public-School Man" in *Decline and Fall* or, in *Men at Arms,* "Apthorpe Gloriosus," Apthorpe Furibundus," and "Apthorpe Immolatus." In *A Handful of Dust,* which has seven chapters numbered consecutively, the repetition of "English Gothic" three times and the slight variation from "Du Côté de Chez Beaver" to "Du Côté de Chez Todd' indicates that the reader should see the episodes in some relationship to one another.

Waugh also included in most of his book-length fiction episodes (he called them epilogues in only four of fourteen novels) that serve as codas to the action and undercut its value by putting it into a larger physical and temporal context. Thus in the "Epilogue" of *Decline and Fall* Paul Pennyfeather returns to the situation he occupied in the "Prelude," wise enough to avoid the disaster that befell him the first time but otherwise changed, if at all, in ways that the author carefully avoids describing. The "Happy Ending" of *Vile Bodies* takes place "on the biggest battlefield in the history of the world."[25] It follows but is not clearly caused by the behavior of the Bright Young People and their elders in the body of that novel.

The earlier novels move primarily in space and subordinate or deny the effects of time, implying that however people move about, they do not essentially change. Not until *Put Out More Flags* (1942), the novel that preceded *Brideshead*, did Waugh use external structure to suggest a movement in time. In a way, then, the external structure of *Brideshead Revisited*—prologue, book 1, book 2, epilogue—represents nothing new for Waugh. That structure and its innovative qualities are easier to see in the contents of the first English edition of 1945 (repeated, with divisions into three rather than two books, in the 1960 revised edition but not included in any American edition):

CONTENTS

Brideshead Revisited

PROLOGUE

SACRED AND PROFANE MEMORIES OF CAPTAIN CHARLES RYDER

Book One

ET IN ARCADIA EGO

Chapter One: *I meet Sebastian Flyte—and Anthony Blanche—I visit Brideshead for the first time*

Chapter Two: *My cousin Jasper's Grand Remonstrance—a warning against charm—Sunday morning in Oxford*

Chapter Three: *My father at home—Lady Julia Flyte*

Chapter Four: *Sebastian at home—Lord Marchmain abroad*

[End of Book One, beginning of Book Two, manuscript version]

Chapter Five: *Autumn in Oxford—dinner with Rex Mottram and supper with Boy Mulcaster—Mr. Samgrass—Lady Marchmain at home—Sebastian contra mundum*

[End of book 1, beginning of book 2, 1960 edition]

Shaping Experience

BRIDESHEAD REVISITED

The title itself suggests other changes in Waugh's approach to fiction. Earlier novels presented characters who returned to settings with the implication that like Paul Pennyfeather at Oxford and William Boot at his country home, they were there to stay and that they would not change further. "Revisited" throws the emphasis from the place to the visit, perhaps implying a greater degree of volition and the possibility that the visitor has changed. At any rate, this title is far more active than the working title, "A Household of the Faith." Moreover, the use of "sacred" in the subtitle, an entirely new element in a novel by Evelyn Waugh, indicates a kind of division if not a complexity that the novel as a whole promised to resolve.

The problem of creating an external structure to attain this goal was so difficult for Waugh that he devised three different ways of dividing the novel. The differences among the three divisions reveal the problems that Waugh and all novelists face. In broad structural terms, he knew from the time he began the novel that it would have a prologue and an epilogue with a real progression between the two. But while he knew fairly precisely what would happen in the body of the novel, he remained uncertain about its structure. Up to the time he finished the handwritten manuscript (for the sake of convenience, I will call this the 1944 version), he planned a three-book structure. The second book consisted of the last four chapters (chapters 5–8) of what became book 1 of the first English edition and all American editions. By the time the novel was in print (the 1945 version), he had decided on the two-book structure. And when he prepared *Brideshead* for the collected edition of his novels (the 1960 version), he created a different three-book structure: the first five chapters in book 1, "Et in Arcadia Ego," the next three in book 2, "Brideshead Deserted," and those in "A Twitch upon the Thread" unchanged except for the numbering as book 3.

There are, of course, many principles of organization (cause-effect; before and after; beginning, middle, end) and many kinds of symmetry (mathematical, chronological, psychological, emotional, physical), and like many artists Waugh worked to make the two principles coincide. The 1944 and 1945 structures, in terms of numbers of chapters per book, were not mathematically symmetrical: 4/4/5 and 8/5. But book 1 of the 1944 version has the advantage of ending with the dramatic pause after the trip to Venice, which marks the end of Charles's idyll with Sebastian; and book 2 begins with a new school year, maintains a somber mood, and moves toward dispersal and decline.

In structuring the 1960 edition, Waugh seems to have considered physical and dramatic symmetry at the expense of chronological balance. The 1944 structure has a rough page count of 84/119/117 for the three books; the 1945 edition is 201/117. Most symmetrical of all is the 1960 edition, 128/75/117, with a 5/3/5 division of chapters. Furthermore, this version includes the entire Oxford sequence in book 1 and puts in book 2 what is essentially reported, offstage action. However, this division leaves disproportionate gaps between books 1 and 2 (June–December of one year) and between book 2 and 3 (ten years).

Of course, the only version that American readers have ever had (and the English had for fifteen years) is divided into two books. In structuring the 1945 version, Waugh apparently looked past advantages of mathematical symmetry to the structural problem of the novel as a whole. The most obvious chronological division in the novel is the ten-year gap between Ryder's taking leave of Marchmain House and the action of "A Twitch upon the Thread." The action on either side of this gap takes roughly three years— 1923 to 1926; 1936 to 1939.

Waugh also had artistic grounds for using a structure that emphasizes two major movements in the novel and that is not extensively modified in the structural patterns of 1944 and 1960. The titles of the two books, "Et in Arcadia Ego" and "A Twitch upon the Thread," emphasize the contrast between the movements. The first, emphasizing the profane half of the novel's subtitle, is classical in origin and frame of reference, is defined in terms of space and is essentially static, and is centered upon the self or ego. The second, emphasizing the sacred, is modern, is defined in terms of extension and movement, separation and reunion, and suggests the relationship between those at either end of the thread.

By contrasting with and complementing each other, the two books support the theme of the novel, and—linked by a web of literary allusions that establish shadings in tone—help to give it form. "*Et in Arcadia Ego*" ("And I [too] am in Arcadia"), which also appears on the skull in Charles's room, has wider and more complex associations. Though the name was taken from a real district of Greece, in classical times Arcadia was used as the setting of pastoral poetry, a highly artificial world in which shepherds ("pastors") languished through idealized and frequently unrequited love affairs, competed with one another in music and poetry, and never encountered real sheep, social problems, or (except in a special form, the pastoral elegy) the ravages of time and change. In Shakespeare's *As You Like It,* for example, the characters Sylvius and Phebe are based on pastoral conventions. Pastoral poetry could criticize the real world because it was separate from the real world, like Peter Pan's "Never, Never Land" and a good deal of science fiction.

Yet Arcadia could only have meaning in contrast to the world of time, change, and death. A number of Renaissance paintings depict pastoral scenes that include a skull bearing this Latin sentence, in order to incorporate death into what seems peaceful and timeless to the casual or uninstructed viewer.[26] At the age of nineteen, Charles is showing his erudition rather than implying his awareness of the instability of his Arcadian, pastoral happiness. He believes, and Sebastian hopes with increasing uncertainty, that they can remain in this world.

The Arcadian world is associated with the "enclosed and enchanted garden . . . not overlooked by any window" (311) which Charles hopes to find when he first goes to Sebastian's rooms and which shuts behind him (169) when he leaves Brideshead in disgrace with Lady Marchmain.[27] This movement from entry to exile, from enclosed security to dispersal, gives shape to the events and the major metaphors of book 1.

Book 2 reverses that pattern. "A Twitch upon the Thread," as Cordelia explains to Charles near the end of book 1, comes from G. K. Chesterton's popular stories, *The Wisdom of Father Brown*, in which the priest-detective catches the thief "with an unseen hook and an invisible line which is long enough to let him wander to the ends of the world and still to bring him back with a twitch upon the thread" (220). This Cordelia reads as a metaphor of God's drawing the wandering sinner back to His love by means of grace. And in fact, in book 2 what was lost is found; what was dispersed through the characters' worldly desires is regathered into the spiritual fold—but not as man without grace would desire. The Good Shepherd, one of the images Christ used to describe Himself, has nothing to do with the pastoral world.

The contrasting movements, outward and inward, are easier to detect because of the external structure, but in themselves they are formal rather than structural principles of order because they work upward from specific characters and events. In this loose sense, form is inductive, working from the particular to the general, while structure is deductive, starting with a generalization or a pattern (like Waugh's adaptation of the external structure of *Decline and Fall* for *Brideshead*) and fitting details into it.

In practice, form and structure are not mutually exclusive. The movements just described as formal are created and reinforced by patterns that Waugh established within the novel and then underlined—for English readers—by the structural device of the chapter headings given above. In them he repeated phrases like "Sebastian contra mundum" and established oppositions like "home" and "abroad" and parallels like "Samgrass revealed" and "Rex revealed." And these are only a few of the comparisons and contrasts—others include Jasper and Anthony Blanche and Julia and Celia—which are Waugh's most characteristic formal principle. By creating unstable and progressive oppositions, he establishes a pattern in which characters complement, contradict, and qualify one another, and he creates a form in which the process of incorporating experience and reconciling then and now, there and here, is more important than any mere succession of events.

Of course novelists can impose structure only upon material that they have formulated or are in the process of formulating. Decisions about structure, form, development, style, character, plot, and point of view take place in rapid succession if not simultaneously; each choice precludes or influences a number of other choices; and no decision can be final until the whole structure is completed. Up to this point, for the sake of convenience, larger principles of organization have been discussed in isolation. Now, to understand more clearly the ways in which Waugh gave shape to experience, it is necessary to consider the questions of whose experience Waugh is portraying and how it is represented.

6

"I am not I":
Actor, Narrator, Author

W augh recognized that his readers would raise the issue of "whose experience" was being represented in the novel. The "Author's Note"— "I am not I; thou art not he or she; they are not they"—is a warning (widely ignored) not to identify the novel's characters with living people. But the first clause can also mean that, while Waugh did not want Ryder to be identified as Waugh, he did not want Waugh to be identified too closely with Ryder. Still further, given the conventions of narrating fiction in the past tense, it is possible to intepret the clause as saying that the "I" of Charles Ryder as the teller of the story is not the same as the "I" of the Charles Ryder who lives through the action. Waugh did not talk about these subtler distinctions, but he worked in a literary context in which they were regarded as important and unavoidable.

The issue of "whose experience" is presented has always been important in narrative literature, and it has been especially important in the practice and theory of fiction over the past hundred years. Popular narrative of all ages and in all genres presents action rather than experience: heroes and heroines may use information to overcome obstacles or to pass tests, but they are not really changed by what they encounter. More complex and consciously artful narrative shifts the emphasis from event to interpretation. The interpreter may be a narrator who exists outside the action with varying degrees of knowledge and control of events and motives. Or the interpreter may be a narrator who is also a character with either a central role as autobiographer, such as Daniel Defoe's Robinson Crusoe or Moll Flanders, or a peripheral role as observer of others' actions, such as Joseph Conrad's Marlow in *Lord Jim* and *Heart of Darkness,* or F. Scott Fitzgerald's Nick Carraway in *The Great Gatsby.* In first person narrative, the teller has no control over events and limited knowledge of them. As in the case of theories of genre, these distinctions merely indicate rather than determine what authors can do with point of view, and it is worth emphasizing once again that no one technique exists in isolation from the others.

Point of view is a particularly important technique in *Brideshead Revisited* because it is the only complete novel in which Evelyn Waugh used a first person narrator. His attitude toward this method of narration changed sharply during his career.[28] Until 1939, when Waugh began and abandoned the story he called *Work Suspended,* he had used an objective and impersonal narrator not only to stand apart from the characters and limit the reader's emotional response to them, but also to bridge major shifts in space and time—in fact, to exercise, subtly but definitely, control of the structure and movement of his novels. *Work Suspended* was narrated by John Plant, a writer of mystery stories who undergoes a series of displacements that force him to face if not accept adulthood. He also comments on the tastes, politics, and habits of his generation and on the way in which it continues or abandons earlier traditions.

Unlike earlier Waugh characters, Plant interprets, synthesizes, and speculates about events, ideas, and feelings. And in using Charles Ryder as the narrator of *Brideshead Revisited,* Waugh drew upon and developed what he had learned in writing *Work Suspended.* Like Plant, Ryder comments on and analyzes his personal past and that of his generation, but in the later novel the social, chronological, and emotional range is wider because, as narrator, Ryder has a slightly different role than does John Plant. Although Plant comments on the activities of his friends, the plot (as far as it goes) concentrates on his activities, and he is not only the focus of the action, he is the central character in the action. Waugh indicated after he finished *Brideshead* that Ryder had a different role. Nancy Mitford, Waugh's friend and fellow novelist, complained that Charles Ryder was "dim." Waugh admitted that she was right but went on to explain that Rdyer was, and had to be, because "he is telling the story and it is not his story." But he went on to identify the "crucial question" as "does Julia's love for him seem real or is he so dim that it falls flat; if the latter the book fails plainly" (*Letters,* 196). Critics tend to doubt that it is possible for a novel with a first person observer not to be about that person, because even if, as in *Heart of Darkness* and *The Great Gatsby,* the narrator observes the actions of others, his process of observation is itself an action. (For the sake of convenience, the actor will be called "Charles," the narrator "Ryder.")

Like most complications in art, this one can be turned to advantage. First person narrators are by definition limited not only to what they can perceive but to the way in which they can perceive it; and as Huckleberry Finn demonstrates, limitations can be useful to the author. For one thing, because the narrator is as ignorant of certain customs, situations, and ideas as the reader, background information can justifiably be explained to both at once. Also, in complex narratives the way in which the narrator learns is as significant as what he or she learns; therefore the reader can be induced to accept not just information but a whole way of seeing.

Even if the first person narrator serves as a mere recording device, Waugh's comment to Mitford indicates that the narrator is selected and given traits that serve the needs of the novel as a whole. In *Brideshead* Waugh wished to evoke understanding rather than, as in earlier novels, judgment, and doing so required a considerable amount of exposition about the events, customs, and institutions I discussed in chapter 4: Oxford University, English history and social structure, and Roman Catholic doctrine and practice. Therefore, Waugh's narrator had to be placed well enough socially and economically to attend Oxford, to have a choice of careers, and to move among the wealthy and high born without arousing attention. On the other hand, he had to be unfamiliar enough with the Flytes' customs and especially their religion to make it plausible for other characters to explain things that the narrator and the audience need to know. Waugh had a theological as well as an artistic purpose in writing the novel, and it was very useful to have the narrator, with whom the audience would identify, reach conclusions by the process that the novelist wanted his readers to follow and outgrow or reject those which he wanted his readers to abandon.

Because in *Brideshead Revisited* Waugh was attempting to encapsulate and interpret England between the two world wars, Charles Ryder has to have certain characteristics. To witness the events of the novel, he needs a certain kind of social standing. He is a gentleman—in England acceptable, though not equal, to the aristocracy—and the son of a gentleman whose elder brother, cousin Jasper's father, lives in a country house with a minstrel's gallery, and thus seems to be a member of the landed gentry.

By the financial standards of the circles that Charles frequents, Charles's family is well off but not wealthy. Unlike most younger sons in English fiction, Charles's father apparently has no financial problems. He has an independent income—which, translated, means that he lives from inherited and invested money and need not hold a job— at least sufficient to allow him to indulge his hobbies and to give Charles the very best education and a very generous living allowance. As he points out to Charles, however, this money "comes out of capital" (25); thus Charles's inheritance will not maintain him in a style equal to that of his father. Therefore, though this is delicately implied rather than crudely specified, Charles will have to do something to earn a living, although during his Oxford career he need not feel, or be, economically inferior even to members of the aristocracy.

Charles has received an expensive education as a matter of course. His public school career—not, alas, at Eton—was blameless and unadventurous, preparing him for the company of "a small circle of college intellectuals, who maintained a middle course of culture between the flamboyant 'aesthetes' [Anthony Blanche, for example] and the proletarian scholars who scrambled fiercely for facts in the lodging houses" (27) and otherwise do not figure in the novel. He is easily diverted from their company and from a vague academic future because, though neither lazy nor stupid, he seems to have little intellectual curiosity or ambition for a career of any kind. In this he is unremarkable at Oxford in the early 1920s and would be unremarkable at most American universities in the late twentieth century.

His religious background, such as it is, is also normal enough. English public schools were founded under religious auspices and at least in Waugh's and Charles's time required students to attend Anglican services. Charles's attitude, acceptable and even normal in his society, is that of the average casual agnostic:

> The view implicit in my education was that the basic narrative of Christianity had long been exposed as a myth, and that opinion was now divided as to whether its ethical teaching was of present value, a division in which the main weight went against it; religion was a hobby which some people professed and others did not; at the best it was slightly ornamental, at the worst it was the province of "complexes" and "inhibitions"—catchwords of the decade—and of the intolerance, hypocrisy, and sheer stupidity attributed to it for centuries. (85–86)[29]

He knows little about the Flytes' Catholicism, and he thinks that it serves only to make them needlessly unhappy.

In all social, external respects, Charles seems to be an average, sensual, upper-middle-class Englishman, U rather than Non-U, with no worries about becoming an insider because, by birth and upbringing, he has always been inside. Looked at subjectively rather than objectively, however, Charles is very much the outsider, oddly passive, disinclined to disagree openly with even the most outrageous suggestions. His lack of self-assertion, his dimness (in Nancy Mitford's terms), makes him a very useful observer of a scene and a good listener to others' monologues in somewhat the same way that Paul Pennyfeather is in *Decline and Fall*. But Charles is characterized much more fully than Paul, and Waugh not only accounts for the causes of his passivity but uses it to support major themes in the novel.

Although Waugh detested psychoanalysis and indeed psychology (see Charles's asides, quoted in the discussions of his religious background), he clearly thought Charles was emotionally stunted by his mother's death and his father's oddness. A family, Charles explains, is "not a thing I know about" (39). Instead, he comments, "I had lived a lonely childhood and a boyhood straitened by war and overshadowed by bereavement; to the hard bachelordom of English adolescence, the premature dignity and authority of the school system, I had added a sad and grim strain of my own" (44–45). As this passage implies, Charles knows nothing about families, about girls, or about love. He goes on to say that Sebastian's company seems to give him "a brief spell of what I had never known, a happy childhood," and in extravagance and even sin he feels "something of nursery freshness about us that fell little short of the joy of innocence" (45). In that company, Oxford seems pastoral; Brideshead seems paradisal. Because Sebastian is aristocratic and the settings are luxurious, Charles's desire to be inside can seem (and sometimes, on the part of the actor-Charles, is) snobbish, but the external trappings are, in terms of the novel, less important than the intensity of Charles's longing for a world in which he can feel at home.

To find that world, however, both Charles in the body of the narration and Ryder in the frame-story have to regress emotionally before they can progress. Charles's love of Sebastian (which is not specifically or primarily homosexual—Sebastian seems to be in what Freud would call the pregenital stage) allows him to return to an earlier stage, to share, in effect, Sebastian's teddy bear and Nanny. In the imagery of the novel, that love gains him entry into "that low door in the wall . . . which opened on an enclosed and enchanted garden" (31)—in which he can feel as well as be an insider.

Through Sebastian Charles also finds a substitute family, and instead of a low door to a secluded pastoral world, he encounters a very large door into what seems for a time to be a much wider world. Lady Marchmain seems to be an unsatisfactory mother-figure; Bridey seems to be a Catholic version of cousin Jasper; and Julia seems, despite her age, to be a superior and disapproving older sister. But Cordelia's energy and enthusiasm and her ready acceptance of Charles make him feel a real part of the family, while Lord Marchmain appears to offer an ideal model of aristocratic masculine style.

Like most of us, Charles uses these models to imagine images, scenarios, or private myths to aid him in getting from where he perceives himself to be to where he thinks he wants to go. The two most important images—one, pastoral Oxford, fully developed; the other, Brideshead as "a world of its own of peace and love and beauty" (321), less clearly defined—enable him to imagine that he is no longer outside, lost and uncertain, but inside, safe and secure.

Yet that shift is the only movement in these rather static conceptions of idealized existence, the first destroyed by the effects of time, the second by conceptions of eternity. More active are the various myths of the Intellectual, the Artist, and the Warrior by which Charles breaks out of the enclosed spaces that fail him. The active myths fail him too, and not until he is able to combine image and action, ideal and practice, are his story and his identity as Charles Ryder complete.

The first of these active myths, that of the Intellectual, has power over his imagination and his life only until he meets Sebastian. The second, that of the Warrior, is so fragmented that most readers have not recognized that it operates in the novel. But Ryder notes in the prologue his youthful, romantic attachment to stories of heroes and battles, and he and Mulcaster share the longing to prove to those who died in the First World War that they too are men. Near the end of the novel Ryder makes a point of telling Lord Marchmain that in the coming war he will be a combat officer rather than an official artist. Finally, in chronological terms, though it is the first thing we learn about Ryder in the novel, he realizes that the myth of glorious service in war offers him no further guidance or consolation.

The third myth, that of the Artist, is translated into fact and controls his life if not his imagination until Lord Marchmain returns to die. There are various versions of the myth. Anthony Blanche tempts him with the pattern of the avant-garde artist, seeking new techniques and new sensations, as a specific against what Blanche regards as the ineffectual and rather vacuous world of the Flytes. Later Charles tells himself that he will "live in a world of three dimensions—with the aid of my five senses" (169), and after living a version of the Bohemian plot in Paris and undertaking his first major painting, he reaches his most expansive point: "I had felt the brush take life in my hand that afternoon; I had had my finger in the great, succulent pie of creation. I was a man of the Renaissance that evening—of Browning's Renaissance. I, who had walked the streets of Rome in Genoa velvet and had seen the stars through Galileo's tube, spurned the friars with their dusty tomes and their sunken, jealous eyes and their crabbed hair-splitting speech" (222). Later he is less certain of his creative power, but he continues to interpret Julia and his affair with her as though both were material for painting and drama (291) until her anger forces him to abandon this way of thinking.

Of course, Charles not only thinks about being an artist, he is an artist, and in financial terms he is quite successful. By the beginning of book 2, however, he has begun to doubt that he has much more to offer than technical proficiency. He does not deny, in fact he seems to welcome, Anthony Blanche's blanket condemnation of the paintings in what, within the framework of the novel, seems to be his final exhibition. Waugh told Nancy Mitford that Ryder was a bad painter in the same way that their friend Sir Osbert Sitwell was a bad writer, perhaps meaning that his obsession with a narrow vision of the past was conveyed in a style too elaborately worked (*Letters*, 196).

In view of this attitude towards Charles's painting, one might ask why Waugh made him an artist at all. As usual, several answers are possible. First, at three points in the novel—in drawing the fountain at Brideshead, in painting Marchmain House, and in doing the portraits of Julia—Charles successfully unites the image that obsesses him and the active principle that animates him or, in other words, fuses feeling and form, vision and technique. These momentary successes give him a further goal and a standard of judging his progress.

Second, as I pointed out in chapter 5, Waugh has adapted the form of the künstlerroman. In novels such as George Moore's *Confessions of a Young Man* and Lawrence Durrell's *The Alexandria Quartet,* the novelist-character may have a creative block or follow mistaken theories. These novels end with the writer's setting down what in effect are the first words of the book we are just finishing. In other words, the book itself is the climax and justification of the artist's process of development. *Brideshead* uses a similar process of artistic development as a principle of organization and serves as a whole to embody the result of that process, but it also uses patterns of emotional and spiritual development to augment and finally to transcend considerations of art.

Third, Waugh makes Charles an artist in order to dramatize his love of human creations and his celebration of them in art as good in themselves. But Waugh indicated quite clearly that technique alone is not enough, and by making the final expression of Ryder's progress not painting but narrative, not art but a religious vision of human destiny, he shifts from the secular level to the sacred. Ryder has not finished his progress any more than "George Moore" or Darley has finished a literary career, but he has, like the narrator of Philip Roth's *Portnoy's Complaint,* reached a point at which he can begin. Although Ryder may never practice his art again, Waugh once argued that art differs "not at all from gardening or needlework [or, like Lord Brideshead, collecting matchboxes?] or any other activity" (*Letters,* 305). This may seem excessive to modern humanists, but Christian poets had long used the palinode or renunciation to turn away from the vanity of secular work to the contemplation of God.

From the vantage point of the end of the novel, we can more readily see that the Ryder who tells the story must be distinguished from the Ryder who tells himself the story about the Intellectual or the Artist or the Warrior. Narrator-Ryder recognizes that the worldly myths have brought actor-Charles to a state of disillusionment which he reaches at several stages in the novel, including the prologue, in which he is outside and sees no way of getting inside. But by consciously reconstructing his past, selecting and arranging incidents and characters, he comes to understand the way in which his worldly talents and earthly loves have brought him to the point at which he can go from the artistically appalling chapel not back into Brideshead, the refuge he had desired for so long, but into the modern, military world with a new spirit and a new hope. To put it another way, the contemplation of his past allows him to function in the world but not to be of it or oppressed by it.

It is obviously difficult for a novelist to juggle the voices of the various "I's" involved in this kind of narrative technique. Although the actor-I may have ideas and attitudes and may commit acts that the narrator criticizes or is ashamed of, the younger self gradually becomes the older self and therefore cannot be rejected entirely. Sometimes the narrator must state what the actor thought or felt; sometimes what the narrator thought or felt; sometimes what they both have always thought or felt; sometimes the way in which the one became or blended into the other. The novelist must manage the voices so that the actor does not seem hopelessly immature and the narrator insufferably superior, and the author must make transitions from one to another to keep the narrative moving in ways that help to establish character and support theme. The only ways to solve these problems are by unremitting attention to style and arrangement of incidents. *Brideshead Revisited,* or any other novel, succeeds only to the degree that the author has imagined and controlled the materials incident by incident, sentence by sentence. The chapters that follow will examine that process.

7

Prologue:
Laying the Foundations

Evelyn Waugh once suggested that the term "architectural" was preferable to "creative" for describing writers because "what makes a writer, as distinct from a clever and cultured man who can write, is an added energy and breadth of vision which enables him to conceive and complete a structure" (*Essays,* 238). To extend the metaphor to *Brideshead Revisited,* in the prologue Waugh faced the problems of building a well-proportioned room, integrating it with the other rooms in his structure, and furnishing it. In literal terms, the prologue as a separate unit required him to establish the character of Charles Ryder, to involve him in a series of situations that cohered in a dramatic structure, and to provide a physical context by which Ryder's mind is created and reflected.

But of course the prologue is not a separate unit. Early in this century Ford Madox Ford and Joseph Conrad worked out a theory of fiction that stated, among much else, that every word of every sentence must contribute to the total effect of the novel, that "the opening paragraph of the book or story should be of the tempo of the whole performance."[30] Waugh never thought highly of Conrad, and he seems never to have mentioned Ford, but even if the prologue of *Brideshead Revis-*

ited does not follow these principles, it certainly illustrates them. In fairly obvious ways the prologue presents the ideas that will dominate the novel and shows the way in which Charles Ryder orders and evaluates his experience. In more subtle fashion the prologue anticipates the narrative pattern and thematic conclusion of the whole novel.

Because the novel is told in Charles Ryder's voice, it is convenient to begin with Waugh's characterization of him. The character in the prologue seems to have little in common with the character I discussed in the previous chapter because the prologue gives us very little information about his social or financial position or his personal past. We learn that he is emotionally sterile, socially isolated, and professionally unfulfilled. His relationship with the army is like a loveless marriage, held together by habit and duty; his former peers have been replaced by younger conscripts of a lower social class (beer and listening to the wireless [radio] are non-U) and his original commanding officer, a kind of father-figure and rallying point, has been replaced by a spit-and-polish martinet obsessed with the letter of military regulations rather than the spirit of combat; and his career, consisting of meaningless movements and training for combat with no enemy in view, has reached a dead end. His memory is limited at first to the three months spent at the camp near Glasgow and then to his four years of his army service. He is like a prisoner in solitary confinement, and three lines from the end of the prologue he refers to his condition and circumstances as "my dungeon."

Waugh contrasts the language of the imprisoned actor-Charles with that of the narrator-Ryder to suggest a world outside. The actor speaks largely in monosyllabic words (only three are longer than two syllables) combined into simple sentences and fragments, and then only to ask questions or give information about military duties. The narrator's style has far wider resources of vocabulary, sentence rhythm, analytic skill, and emotional range. All of these indicate possibilities that are for the moment left unexplored. For example, the extended comparison of the army with marriage (5–6) contains a series of negations of desire, tenderness, pleasure, curiosity, and so on, but each of these negations implies a positive value from which, at this point, he is cut off.

The incidents of the prologue establish in more obvious ways actor-Charles's isolation from both higher and lower ranks. The only emotion he reveals is a sneaking sympathy for Hooper after the hair-cutting episode, used primarily to set off the scene at the trash-filled ditch when he senses that the colonel thinks of him in much the same way that Charles thinks of Hooper. But Waugh uses these parallel scenes to point up important differences in character. Ryder, unjustly blamed, embarrasses the colonel; Hooper accepts his rebuke without resentment and even with a kind of humility. The effects of the behavior are predictable: the colonel, stung, assigns extra duty to Ryder and his company in the vindictive hope of further demonstrating Ryder's incompetence; Ryder, more tolerant or less a bastard than he sounds, assigns the easiest jobs to Hooper in the desire to discover a task that he can accomplish.

As narrator, Ryder presents the colonel and Hooper in visual terms as caricatures: moustache, hairstyle, accents, tone of voice, and other details define them and deny complexity. Also, he thinks of them as stereotypes of their class and status: the colonel is a peevish school-master, Hooper is a provincial, lower middle-class clerk and archetype of Youth. By placing them in these categories, he can see and judge them more clearly and by implication contrast them unfavorably with himself and with ideals of soldierly behavior.

Categorizing and contrasting are the most significant means by which Ryder perceives. He needs to establish definite boundary lines for himself, and he maintains a superior attitude toward those who cannot do so, notably the colonel, who cannot distinguish the boundary between platoon areas, and Hooper, who asks lamely, "How am I to find the perimeter in the dark?" The "planless maze" (7) of the army camp offends him as much as it would Alexander Pope, from whose lines about "this *Scene* of *Man* / A Mighty Maze! but not without a Plan" (*Essay on Man*, Epistle 1,11.5–6) Waugh adapted the phrase. In direct contrast is Ryder's description of Brideshead's "simple, carefully designed pattern. . . . planned and planted a century and a half ago [in Pope's lifetime] so that, at about this date, it might be seen in its maturity" (16).

Prologue

Between the view of the camp and the view of Brideshead, both seen from above, Waugh uses Ryder to present a variety of contrasts to suggest abstract values and to prepare for the shift from the planless to the planned. The end of paved road a quarter mile from the camp marks the difference between civilian slackness and military discipline. Farmhouse, pasture, and orchard are better than the suburb that will replace them. The "noble gates" of the madhouse contrast with the "rough wire" of the camp, but the period before the "century of progress" is better than the present, and the progressive, utilitarian education of Hooper is inferior in content and effect to the literary and historical public school education of Ryder. Purpose is superior to drift, enchantment to routine, love to duty, volunteer officer to conscript [draftee], moist to dry. The natural is better than the human and any sound is better than radio broadcasts.

The emotional weight with which Ryder invests these opposed pairs comes from two more general contrasts involving time and space—then and now, here and there—which serve as major structural principles in the novel and which, resolved into unity, serve as major formal principles. "Here" is obvious: the word begins five of the first nine paragraphs. Ryder hates "here" for reasons that he makes quite clear, but, for most of the prologue, he cannot imagine the complement or opposite, "there," and is ignorant of and incurious about the destination of his unit. He is able to imagine a "then" as well as a "now," but there is not, to use a photographic analogy, much depth of field between present and past, so that he can gain no perspective. To him, at this point, "then," which in common usage can mean either "before" or "next," signifies to him only the past. To him, the future is merely another camp and more meaningless training or a period so remote that archeologists can only struggle vainly to interpret the conditions of his present.

Waugh establishes the key concepts that govern Ryder's picture of the world in the two opening paragraphs:

> When I reached C Company lines, which were at the top of the
> hill, I paused and looked back at the camp, just coming into full

view below me through the grey mist of early morning. We were leaving that day. When we marched in, three months before, the place was under snow; now the first leaves of spring were unfolding. I had reflected then that, whatever scenes of desolation lay ahead of us, I never feared one more brutal than this, and I reflected now that it had no single happy memory for me.

Here love had died between me and the army. (3)

Some terms, like "here" and "then," are explicitly used; some, like "there" ("leaving that day"), are implied.

However, the passage does more than present key terms. Roughly in order of complexity, it anticipates, as I have already pointed out, the perspective from which Ryder will see the landscape of Brideshead at the end of the prologue; it presents Ryder as detached and passive (note the intransitive verbs in the main clause, "paused" and "looked"); it suggests the division of Ryder the narrator from Charles the actor; it establishes the link between physical and psychic geography, what Ryder sees and how he feels about it; it presents in miniature ("I paused and looked back") the retrospective, nonchronological narrative order in the prologue and in the whole novel; and it indicates the possibility of change and development and the means by which they will occur.

This may seem to be an excessive burden for a single paragraph to bear, even a paragraph composed by an "architectural" writer, but of course readers as well as writers take advantage of hindsight and use evidence from the whole text to rewrite or reread. But for writers as well as readers that whole is made up of parts, and in the best work the parts not only fit together but also help to shape our understanding of the whole. In other words, we cannot understand the full weight of a single paragraph until we have seen the pattern of the whole text, but we cannot see that pattern without hints from paragraph after paragraph.

For example, the structure of the novel's opening sentence, quoted above, is rather complex: the movement from "when" to the implied "then" is interrupted by a descriptive clause, and the end, a long prepositional phrase, is anticlimactic. The next short sentence moves forward, but the third turns to the past. In itself, this pattern would not mean much, but Waugh uses the same hesitant forward and backward movement in longer units of narrative in the prologue and throughout the novel. Thus, after the opening action ("reached"), Ryder stands atop the hill reflecting until, four pages later, he speaks to the sergeant-major. When Hooper appears the forward action is suspended for two more pages while Ryder describes and evaluates him.

These and other shifts from narrative to reflective and expository passages and back again are made clear by transitional phrases even though the material is chronologically discontinuous. On pages 11 and 15 Waugh employs a different kind of apparent discontinuity by using white space to divide one section from another. The first break separates the sergeant major's statement of conventional wisdom about annoying senior officers from the march past the madhouse. The second break separates Ryder's arrival at his new quarters from his waking. Both breaks emphasize underlying similarities: between the army and the asylum and between Ryder's physical and spiritual exhaustion.

These narrative devices create local, structural connections, but larger patterns are needed to give form to the prologue as a whole. The major pattern, which opens new perspectives in space and time, is introduced in the progression from winter to spring mentioned in the first paragraph. In most traditions, including the Christian tradition, the coming of spring symbolizes the movement from death to new life. At the beginning, Ryder turns away from the prospect where "the first leaves of spring were unfolding" to focus on the bitter memories of the past winter. When he reaches Brideshead, however, he looks down at "the beech faintly dusted with green by the breaking buds" and perceives a pattern in the scene before him. This difference between the two descriptions is more than elegant variation to avoid repeating the same words. The first phrase presents information; the second not only creates an aesthetic experience but, in its context as part of a grand design, demonstrates that human activity, including artistic activity, can speak across the centuries to affect the future.

Ryder is able to move to this point because his perspectives of time and space have expanded during the course of the prologue. At the beginning his memory can stretch to cover only the three months spent in camp, and by page 6 it extends only to the four years of his army career. His conception of space is limited to the army camps that have come to seem indistinguishable, a sign of passive despair for a mind given to drawing distinctions, and he is both ignorant of and incurious about the destination of his unit.

In the middle of the prologue, however, he recalls "the age when my eyes were dry to all save poetry—that stoic red-skin interlude which our schools introduce between the fast flowing tears of the child and the man" (9). He now describes himself as "sere [dry, dessicated] and lawless." This phrase, in the context of his earlier distinction about the tears of child and man, may imply that now he is not really a man or perhaps (water and life being traditionally connected) fully alive but in an incomplete and intermediate stage. Even so, his memories of heroic poetry connect him to his boyhood, introducing a wider span of his past and the first pleasant thoughts he articulates.

When, in the last section of the prologue, he learns where he is (we are not told the name and must infer it from the novel's title), he perceives not just expanded and artfully ordered sights and sounds in time and space but, "awed and bemused between two realities and two dreams," a world that provides the alternative of "sweet, natural, and long-forgotten sounds" (15) to the waking frustration-dreams of the wartime world. In referring to the landscape as "still unravished" (16), he moves from heroic to romantic poetry, from action to the kind of contemplation that John Keats practiced in "Ode on a Grecian Urn." When he tells Hooper "I've been here before," he brings together space and time, here and there, then and now, a lovely place, a magical time in a new and healing way that goes beyond nostalgia. The recovery and re-creation of that time and space, from saying that he knows all about it to feeling that knowledge, is a major—but not, as I will demonstrate in discussing the epilogue, the final—purpose of the rest of the novel.

8

Paradise Gained and Lost

The first five chapters of book 1 begin with Charles in Arcadia and present, gradually and with increasing intensity, the difficulties of ignoring the significance of the skull that represents time and decay. Charles can only witness these processes, the complexities of the adult world, and Sebastian's decline; he has no resources with which to oppose them. But the process of decay is very slow, and Waugh takes great care to present the beauty of the world that cannot endure as well as the events that threaten it.

CHAPTER 1

In this chapter, Charles begins to explore the past and the setting—the "here before"—that the return to Brideshead has opened to him. Like the prologue, this chapter uses a trip to Brideshead as an overarching principle of temporal and spatial organization, and like the prologue, the internal form is based not on chronology but on subjective associations that place at the center of the narrative not action but experience and its evaluation. Because the prologue has accustomed the reader to this method and to the voice of Ryder, which establishes a different kind of continuity, in chapter 1 Waugh is able to use a series of paired narrative units that fit one inside the other. (This technique is called frame narration, but the metaphor has obvious limits because, in the first place, the frames have only two sides, and in the second place, they sometimes connect as well as divide.) This technique allows Waugh to control the amount and position of expository detail, to underline a series of contrasting characters and situations, and to reinforce the theme, finally realized in the epilogue, that one must recover the past in order to move into the future.

The construction of the chapter—in ten stages, using four frames, with two contrasting movements—is more complicated in texture and more varied in length and importance than a list can show, but that construction is easiest to follow in a numbered outline:

1. wartime
2. beginning of trip to Brideshead
3. summary of meeting with Sebastian
4. Jasper's advice
5. father's lack of advice
6. Jasper's advice
7. Charles's Oxford career
8. dramatized meeting with Sebastian
9. visit to Brideshead and return
10. wartime

The frames work inward: one and ten, two and nine, three and eight, four and six. Stages three and four occupy only a few lines of text, as if to mark one edge of a space to be filled in later. Unlike most exercises in literary mathematics but like Waugh's practice in *A Handful of Dust,* the pattern is not completely symmetrical: five and seven do not fit. Waugh may have been less interested in mathematics than in a pattern that expands upon the movement of the prologue and the idea—Ryder has to move backward to go forward—which that movement reinforces. Therefore, one through five move further and further into Ryder's past; six through ten move forward again.

Paradise Gained and Lost

Of course, that Waugh constructed his chapter in this way is less interesting than the reasons for which he seems to have done so. Most obviously, he wanted to establish with the first frame both continuity and contrast between 1943 and 1923, and the opening and closing lines of the chapter resemble the fade-in/fade-out technique that moviemakers of his time used to indicate flashbacks. This narrative continuity is important in both fiction and film because thematic continuity, or the relevance of the flashback to the material in the dramatic present, will not be apparent until the flashback ends—in *Brideshead Revisited*, more than three hundred pages later.

The frame-within-a-frame construction of the chapter also permits Waugh to organize his narrative not by chronology but by the principle of contrast that is Ryder's characteristic way of perceiving. In chapter 1 and in the rest of the novel, however, contrast is less a feature of Ryder's narrative style than of the arrangement of characters and events that Charles as actor rather passively observes. Although Ryder as narrator occasionally comments and analyzes, the real significance of the events is a result of their juxtaposition; the connection is left for the reader to make.

The opening half of the second frame, the beginning of the journey to Brideshead, makes contrasts in two directions. Looking back, it repeats the pattern of the prologue, but it also establishes, especially in its first half, major contrasts in tone and texture with the prologue. The journey in the prologue begins at a disorderly and ugly camp where Ryder's "last love died" (5) and takes place at night, in a crowded troop train and under conditions made needlessly uncomfortable by the commanding officer, with meager rations in transit and not even cocoa to look forward to as the unit reaches its quarters in the rain. The journey in chapter 1 begins in rare and glorious sunlight at an Oxford described in terms of art—as an aquatint—and Arthurian romance—as Lyonesse, the legendary home of the Tristan who loved Isolde, now sunk into the sea—from which, well-provisioned and unhurried, Charles' trip is elegantly sponsored by the person for whom his first love is born. Other details set in opposition to those of the prologue include the sergeant major and Lunt, members of a professional class who transmit the lore of the army and of Oxford; the all-male society of soldiers yearning towards women and the all-male society of Oxford outraged by their incursion; Hooper "scarcely human" and slovenly, burdened with his kit and unable to help Ryder, and Sebastian, elegant and languid, hardly straining himself with his cargo of teddy bear, strawberries, and a new wine for Charles to taste.

The end of the first side of this frame may not seem to look forward in dramatic terms, but it does serve as a point of reference for the rest of the chapter because it presents and defines the novel's Arcadian theme as Charles's sensory and emotional response seems to free him from the limitations of space, time, and gravity. Sebastian's reference to age and misery brings them back to earth, and the rest of the chapter presents various kinds of limitations, some irrelevant and some, it is suggested, inescapable.

At this point Waugh uses a blank space to cut from dramatized scene to summary narration of Charles's first meeting with Sebastian in order to frame and subordinate material presented in sections four through seven about Charles's previous life and his prospects for an Oxford career. Within that frame, he introduces cousin Jasper, a pompous careerist who is grave beyond his years ("formally," "heavy," and "gravity" are key words) to provide a framework for Charles's father, frivolous beyond his. The juxtaposition of characters makes both seem more extreme, and therefore funnier, and the placement of the father's nonadvice establishes Charles's motivation, or lack of it, in ignoring Jasper's advice when it finally comes.

In fact, Jasper gives good advice, both shalts and shalt nots, to anyone who wants to be a conventional university success. He also serves as a monument to, or horrible example of, the effect of that advice. Even though Jasper's advice is ignored, it is the structural pivot on which the chapter turns from moving backward in time to moving forward, and the reason for ignoring it—the gillyflowers that bloom under the undesirable windows—looks backward to Charles who lay on the turf smoking and foreshadows the Charles who encounters Sebastian by means of those windows and falls under his spell.

First, however, Charles has to work through his own scenario for an Oxford career by furnishing his room. Even more than in Waugh's other novels, characters in *Brideshead* are defined by their taste, or lack of it, in interior decor. Narrator-Ryder has his vision of how the room should have looked but is honest enough to admit actor-Charles's limited imagination and very cautiously advanced taste (see my discussion of this passage in chapter 1), reflected in the people who—the term indicates Charles's passivity—"adopted" him. His friends, like his tastes, are a logical extension of his past rather than an expansion of it. Collins has more sense of humor and wider learning than Jasper, but as his discussion of aesthetics (28) shows, he grasps the letter rather than the spirit, the idea rather than the emotion.

Sebastian does the opposite, as the same passage indicates, but before Charles can perceive as Sebastian does, he must work through Jasper's latent influence, Collins' dismissive labeling, and Sebastian's vomiting. This last scene shows Waugh at his most skillful. He contrasts the physical and mental atmospheres of stuffy intellectualism with the outdoors; metaphysical discussion with a dinner party; people like Collins, sober in all senses of the word, who have been to the public school Winchester with incoherent (though elegant) people who have been to Eton; undergraduates practicing to be academic intellectuals with those learning to be men of the world. Because Sebastian appears at the windows Jasper disparaged and vomits into the room Collins occupies, throwing up may be a form of criticism. And as the shift in Lunt's attitude about the mess foreshadows—both are impressed by Sebastian's extravagant reparations—it is a criticism that Charles is prepared to accept because, as he indicated earlier, he felt Collins and his circle were "not all that Oxford had to offer" (28).

First, however, the reader must be made to accept Sebastian. The idyllic scene at the beginning of the chapter and Charles's comments about Sebastian in the bridge passage from midnight to the following noon—introducing the central image of "the low door in the wall" to the "enclosed and enchanted garden" (31)—act in his favor, but the luncheon party scene is most clearly calculated to shape attitudes towards him. Waugh ignores the usual practice (Shakespeare's, for example, in *Anthony and Cleopatra*) of using minor characters to prepare for the entrance of the leading actor. The narrator says that Sebastian is beautiful; he gives details about the incongruous furnishings of the room, works of art mingling with mere souvenirs, which reflects the furnishings of Sebastian's mind; Sebastian's dialogue reveals directly, and thus needs no comment, that his conversation is easy and that he is unapologetic about his behavior, about his appetite, and about his teddy bear, which (or who) seems less bizarre than in the first account of him.

Sebastian makes the three Etonian guests seem mannered and snobbish; they in turn make him seem friendly and charming. All, for example, have access to a level of London society not open to Charles, and the three act superior to it. Sebastian is so superior that he does not bother to frequent it. But they are merely a chorus (as they will be explicitly termed in chapter 5; here (38), they are figures on a frieze) or an audience for Anthony Blanche, who has various functions in the novel, including entertainment. Here Blanche serves to define Sebastian as natural, direct, and innocent. (The contrast in their ways of speaking—Sebastian's simple, additive structure and Anthony's stammer used as one device in sentences perfectly timed to surprise and disconcert—is perhaps the most important way of distinguishing between them.) Blanche's taste is very avant-garde: T. S. Eliot's *The Waste Land* had created a scandalous sensation only the year before Anthony reads it from the balcony. He is always showing off, but he puts on an excellent show, and what he says usually has a disquieting grain of truth. Here, for example, though he may be a false prophet, he resembles, in his inversion (or, in a later account, bisexuality), the Tiresias of Greek myth who had lived both as a woman and as a man. And he interprets others in his own peculiar way, correctly identifying Sebastian with the early Christian martyr shot full of arrows while delicately imputing to him the beauty of most Renaissance portraits of that lightly draped and mildly homoerotic figure.

Sebastian's impulse to take Charles to a real garden may seem surprising in view of his luncheon guests, but Waugh uses the brief episode to complete a stage in Charles's education, so that when he returns to his room the flowers that Sebastian has sent make the rest of his room seem artificial. (Charles may also have been shamed by the contrast with Blanche's really advanced taste, but this is less certain.) And the trip to the botanical gardens also has a formal purpose, serving as a transition back to the journey to Brideshead where the narrator-Ryder had left Charles and Sebastian in the natural world (24, 34).

Almost immediately thereafter, the two reach Brideshead in a sentence whose carefully established movements, hesitations, and additions culminates in the view of "a new and secret landscape" (32), the embodiment and expansion beyond every expectation of Charles's dream of the "enclosed and enchanted garden." But Charles is hurried in and out of the magnificent rooms and made to feel like a vulgar tourist because Sebastian can be comfortable only in the simplicity and security represented by Nanny Hawkins, who, like all nannies, including Waugh's, served as a surrogate mother and kept aristocratic and even upper-middle-class children too young for school or governesses out of the parents' way.

The view of Nanny at the window that opens onto the magnificent grounds of Brideshead establishes contrasts that will be important in the last fifty pages: simplicity and grandeur, feeling and style, simple faith and noble blood. At this point, however, she seems rather like home base in Sebastian's private game to which Charles does not know the rules, and the trip to Brideshead leaves him more puzzled than enlightened. He is allowed a full view only of the chapel, to the style of which, if not the spiritual life it implies, Sebastian can feel superior.

Like readers of the novel, Charles is gradually provided with information that Ryder already has, but Waugh and the narrator are tracing the process through which actor became narrator, not extolling the superior judgment of hindsight that would condemn the actor's ignorance rather than reveal the process by which he learns. However, the novel uses two quite different kinds of foreshadowing. The first is dramatic, as when Sebastian mentions that his father is a social leper or when Charles wonders at, though he does not speculate about, Sebastian's uneasiness at Brideshead. A quite different kind of foreshadowing might be called lyric because it uses something like operatic leitmotivs; it uses the voice of the narrator and the experience of the actor to drop hints and suggestions about material that will be developed later. For example, alert readers will know from Hooper's comment in the prologue about the Catholic chapel, "More in your line than mine" (17), that Ryder is at this point a Catholic. In chapter 1, the theme of religion is developed almost subliminally in phrases like Ryder's "glory of God" (21) and in Jasper's view that "religious groups . . . do nothing but harm" (26) before Ryder copies Sebastian's acts of reverence in the chapel (38). And the first hint that Charles or Ryder has any interest in art comes when Sebastian writes a note "in conté crayon on a whole sheet of my choice Whatman H. P. drawing paper" (30)—not the kind of paper the casual sketcher would have on hand.

Waugh's first chapter serves quite traditional functions: introducing characters, providing enough information to allow readers to follow the action and understand motivation, and raising dramatic questions that the remainder of the book will answer. This chapter employs the craftsmanship that Waugh always praised. However, the technique is not simply functional: it shapes the material so that it can say more than direct discourse could.

CHAPTER 2

All good performers, including artists, must have a very sharp sense of timing, and that involves knowing where to start and how to continue— and when to stop, which is well before the audience gets tired of a particular joke, trick, or artistic effect. The best performers know how to introduce new material or effects and at the same time, in unexpected ways, to maintain a link with the old and thereby give a sense that the performance is not just a series of acts, like a variety show, but something that has been given outward structure and internal coherence.

As I demonstrated in chapter 5, Evelyn Waugh had a clear sense of the shape of *Brideshead Revisited* as a whole. But he also had an excellent sense of timing revealed in the rhythms of individual sentences, in rhythms created by sentences placed in juxtaposition or opposition, and, more difficult to perceive and describe, in rhythms of longer units. For example, chapter 1 repeats in more various and far more complex fashion structural elements introduced in the prologue. In chapter 2, Waugh uses a much simpler, essentially chronological method of construction, but he uses enough retrospective narration to sustain the flashback method and the theme that one must move backward in order to move forward.

Chapter 1 emphasizes the new experiences of Charles as actor and uses a highly complex structure to allow Ryder as narrator to evaluate that experience by establishing a context for it. Chapter 2 puts Charles more often in the position of having to evaluate experience for himself. When he is able to do so, his conclusions, though not their form, correspond to the conclusions reached by Ryder.

This different kind of complexity is possible because the chapter is constructed fairly simply. It contains three major scenes—Jasper's "Grand Remonstrance," Anthony Blanche's seduction speech, and Charles's visit to Sebastian—and two bridge passages or interludes—the first giving details to fill in Jasper's outline, the second following Charles through an Oxford Sunday as he goes to find Sebastian. The first scene and interlude look towards the past; the second scene and interlude look towards the future; and the final scene, in which Ryder offers no comment, leaves Charles less sure of the terms with which to evaluate his current experience than he was at the end of the first scene.

Jasper's "Grand Remonstrance" is linked to the past, or a particular aspect of it, and provides a framework for the ensuing flashback. His appearance and his academic struggle with the examinations—which (rather than a grade point average) determine the level and therefore the value of his degree—offer a pattern that Charles might copy. However, Jasper's speech is less a sermon than an indictment—he does not call for repentance and reform, but simply lays out the charges.

Jasper's visit helps to measure Sebastian's effect on Charles's taste in interior decor and on his behavior, and Ryder further emphasizes this effect in the interlude that follows. First he reintroduces Collins, already established as a foil to Sebastian, and the trip to Ravenna, cold as well as "economical and instructive" (cliché terms of puritanical approval that long ago became schoolboy code words for sparseness and tedium), contrasts with the trip to Brideshead just as the style of Collins's acknowledgment contrasts with that of Sebastian's letter. Collins is a little less easily dismissed than Jasper as a model for Charles's Oxford career not merely because he is less absurd but also because of some element inherent in Charles's character.

This element can be explained only by metaphor, an important stylistic element in *Brideshead*. Although Ryder and Waugh disparaged psychology (Waugh once declared that there was no such word), *Brideshead Revisited* is to some degree about processes that can only be termed psychological. Rather than analyze them, Waugh used— very occasionally in earlier novels; fairly often in this one—figures of speech to imply or suggest a complex emotional state. The metaphor introduced at this point offers a clue to the novel's conception of character and its development. Ryder says that the real reason why he did not emulate Collins was that "the hot spring of anarchy rose from deep furnaces where was no solid earth, and burst into the sunlight—a rainbow in its vapours—with a power the rocks could not repress" (44). The image that he presents, called the vehicle of the metaphor, is that of a geyser spouting from below the earth's crust. As usual, the idea being expressed, called the tenor, is much more complex. Neither Waugh nor Ryder seems the type to approve of anarchy in any sense, especially the political sense. However, Waugh had spoken approvingly of anarchy because it involved energy and movement. Here, Ryder seems to be saying that internal energy breaks through conventional enclosures to issue forth in beauty and (if he alludes to the rainbow that marks the end of the deluge in Genesis) consolation. This metaphor is reinforced by another—the blending and maturing of port (45)—which employs images of the movement from darkness to light, from repression to freedom, to establish the idea that apparently unpalatable elements can have good results.

These metaphors surround a paragraph that presents variations of their implications in narrative and thematic terms. Ryder says that he had come to late adolescence without having been a child, and the impulses of childhood issue forth in his revelry with Sebastian. In theological terms, those actions may be sinful, but in regressing, Charles is going through a stage necessary to his ultimate maturation. There is, here and elsewhere in the novel, a very fine line between the orthodox notion that one can be saved even though one sins and the heterodox notion that one must sin in order to be saved; between the idea that God can turn all things to good and the view that therefore everything leads to good. But Charles's character is not ready for decanting, in terms of the port metaphor that follows and that implies a concluding stage not yet reached. This segment concentrates on process, not result, on Charles loving rather than Charles finally transformed by and able to define love, on Charles responding to the gillyflowers rather than to Jasper's stiff and somber figure just as he did in chapter 1.

The narrative method of the interlude is more interesting than its theology, and its chief purpose is to show that Ryder accepts his younger self and refuses (as he also does on pp. 25 and 62) to second-guess his decisions or sophisticate his responses. This narrator-actor relationship is not unique, but it does run counter to the more conventional pattern—exemplified in St. Augustine's *Confessions* and Charles Dickens's *Great Expectations*—in which the narrator emphasizes youthful errors and dramatic conversions. In generic terms, *Brideshead Revisited* is less a confession than an apology—which, in justifying rather than criticizing past behavior, has much in common with the künstlerroman. The pattern in which narrator approves of actor has led some critics, as I pointed out in chapter 3, to identify them completely with each other and with Waugh and to disparage the novel as nostalgic, sentimental, and self-indulgent.

Almost as if Waugh recognized the problem, he has the narrator return to the dramatic present—linking it to the past with the reference to the gillyflowers—and surrender, for the remainder of the chapter, his ability to comment and analyze. Instead, Charles must confront, without support or confirmation from the narrator, a strain on his new sophistication, a threat to his "joy of innocence" and a severe test of the talisman that he uses to repel Jasper.

Anthony Blanche is the antithesis of Jasper in a number of ways: Jasper wants to pull Charles backwards to past forms of conventional righteousness and make him a good Oxford man; Blanche wants to pull Charles forward to new kinds of experience and make him into a homosexual artist of the international avant-garde like all of those mentioned on page 46. Jasper, refusing Charles's champagne, is too dull and English; Blanche, offering Charles Alexander cocktails, is too exciting and rootless. And in the construction of chapter 2, Jasper need only appear and begin to speak because he has already been introduced; Blanche is given a full and formal introduction, so that he occupies more space and carries more weight. Jasper prepares for Blanche's entrance by his disapproving speech; Blanche does not even recognize that Jasper exists.

However, both present Charles with worldly values that do not include knowing and loving another human being, and both are, in their own ways, right. But Anthony is also like Charles: in both the process of development has been arrested or deflected. Charles, in the company of Sebastian, returns to nursery innocence; Anthony, having missed the smoothing and civilizing process of school life, is like a young savage. Charles has to learn to play; Anthony cannot learn to stop fighting. Like Jasper, Blanche cannot change.

But unlike Jasper, Blanche is a threat to Charles's equanimity because he belongs to a world that Charles half wants to enter. In short, he intimidates Charles by making him feel callow and inexperienced. Not surprisingly, he does so primarily with a verbal style that is allusive to people, places, things, languages—while assuming that *of course,* my dear, you know all about it—and beautifully though surprisingly cadenced, sometimes balanced, sometimes elliptical, sometimes parenthetical, and always polished and idiosyncratic. Like a good performer, his timing is impeccable, and in writing his dialogue Waugh revised it more frequently and more extensively than he did that of any other character.[31]

Blanche can also construct what does not at first seem to be a persuasive speech. He begins with a very amusing account of having been dunked in the fountain, substantiating Jasper's factual account but making it into an adventure with himself as the hero. Then he appears to admit inferiority—no one would dunk Sebastian, and Sebastian was not expelled from Eton—while implying that Sebastian is at best passive and at worst treacherous. Then, with no apparent transition, he mentions his cosmopolitan acquaintance (Sebastian, we recall from chapter 1, knows a new wine; Blanche knows the owners of the vineyards) and touches Charles's vanity by calling him an artist; telling him of a famous artist's response; flattering him for not being what he has been afraid of not being: exquisite. Then, having put himself and Sebastian in the same class, he contrasts their responses to Charles's drawings by referring to Aloysius, the teddy bear, in what serves as a kind of litany (see pp. 51, 52, 57, and especially 61) to establish Sebastian as childish and vacuous.

Anthony's next tactic is extremely subtle: he lightly draws the analogy between Sebastian and Stefanie de Vincennes, describes his affair briefly, and moves with apparent casualness to a description of Sebastian's family. (The family name is Flyte; Alex, the father, and Teresa, the mother, are the Marquess and Marchioness of Marchmain and are referred to by their titles.) Then he contrasts Sebastian with the rest of his family and with himself, using, as he had earlier, images of airiness and ephemerality in contrast to gravity and weight to emphasize Sebastian's decorative stupidity. He then implies that as Stefanie was to Anthony, so Sebastian will be to Charles. Therefore, if Charles does not want to become like Anthony, he must. . . . The conclusion is not drawn, but the implication is perfectly clear. And he ends with the prediction that Sebastian will turn any subsequent conversation to his bear.

The second interlude, which follows Blanche's lengthy monologue, does not move, like the first, into Charles's past but continues in Charles's dramatic present to show the nightmarish effect of the speech, to contrast with that effect the Sunday morning world in which the pious go in crowds to worship their deities and Charles goes along to Sebastian and cannot find him because he has another object of devotion.

The final scene—almost entirely in dialogue, without comment or any intervention by the narrator—presents Charles's attempt to verify or disprove Anthony's stories and, less obviously, the implications about Sebastian. Sebastian casually denies or qualifies most of the details—but he substantiates Blanche's final and most emphatic prediction by turning from Charles to Aloysius.

This has two effects: it leaves Charles with new doubts about Sebastian, and it establishes Blanche as a kind of prophet, not merely of this event but also for the whole novel. In fact, his account of the Flyte family has been corroborated by Sebastian's reference to his father as "a social leper" (23) and the rest of his family as charming and by Jasper's account of the Marchmains' separation. His prediction about future stories of his dunking (50) will be fulfilled sooner than he expects (205). More important than any specific prophecy, his descriptions will condition the ways in which Charles, and the reader, will regard each family member when she or he appears in the story.

Chapter 2 ends on a note of dramatic and psychological irresolution, not even posing clear questions that will need to be answered in future chapters. The idyllic mood invoked at the end of chapter 1 and sustained through the first third of this chapter has been dispelled; Charles's confidence in his judgment and in his emotional attachment has been shaken; and dramatic continuity has been interrupted. This may seem a daring move for a novelist, but it establishes the ways— frustration, anticlimax—in which the narrative as a whole will develop.

CHAPTER 3

Chapter 3 continues and culminates the movement from complex to simple structures in the chapters of book 1. It is built on a relatively simple contrast between Charles's physical and psychological confinement—the consequence of his entry into the enchanted garden at Oxford—and his release into an even more secret and opulent version of that garden at Brideshead. In thematic terms, the chapter employs, though in simpler fashion, the here/there contrast established in the prologue and chapter 1, moving from the depressing "here" of the London house of Edward Ryder to the consoling "there" of Brideshead. In dramatic terms, the chapter moves from Charles's low point at the end of chapter 2 to a point still nearer despair and then—like the prologue—takes him to Brideshead to restore his spirits.

The chapter begins with a literal and figurative balance sheet that shows Charles without resources financially, psychologically, and morally. He is also in a position familiar to young people returning home after a perod of independence, neither child nor adult, neither indulged nor independent. Waugh reinforces the sense of confinement by careful selection: Charles is directly presented only within the house—from the windows of which he sees nothing—so that the first section of the chapter has no place but "here." Still, as in previous chapters, Ryder refuses to second-guess his younger self even in his misery. In fact, Ryder uses the image of wisdom as "the last coin of a legacy which dwindles with time" (62) rather than the fruit of individual effort to imply that value is to be found in time passed rather than in time passing and that experience in present time takes us farther from the truth.

Waugh uses Charles's father to demonstrate that ignoring or escaping from time passing is not an acceptable solution. The elder Ryder plays with time as he does with language and with people. He assumes the appearance, walk, and voice of a much older man; his clothes, "a deliberate archaism" (63), are like costumes that ignore or defy the cycle of fashion as Charles cannot ignore the "calculable regularity" of the roulette of remorse; his dinner party is reconstructed from the distant past. By avocation he is an antiquarian (an amateur collector with wide rather than specialized knowledge and tastes) and therefore expends most of his time and attention on the past, ignoring the summer night, the traffic noises, and the clocks that measure time passing. While Charles is confined, his father is free to come and go on mysterious grownup errands, including—as a reminder to Charles of their respective positions—a trip to the zoo where the cages, unlike the house, are open to the sun.

Although the comparison may seem odd at first glance, Edward

Ryder has a good deal in common with Anthony Blanche: he plays games with language; he wears a costume rather than clothes; he orchestrates a dinner with Charles as audience; he delights in unsettling his audience; he has a marvelous, malicious sense of timing; and he has made himself into a kind of caricature as a means of escape or self-defense. Of course, Anthony wants to seduce Charles and Edward wants to get rid of him, but in both cases their artfulness makes Charles look at Sebastian in a more critical fashion. Anthony's criticism is direct; Edward creates an atmosphere (like Collins's Ravenna in chapter 2) from which Charles seeks deliverance.

Sebastian's airy letter, like that of chapter 2, reveals a kind of egotism that is simpler than Anthony's and Edward's but even more painful to Charles because it seems to indicate that Sebastian needs him less than he needs Sebastian. It implies that Sebastian is not going to deliver him from his current plight, and it evokes images of Anthony Blanche's face and words and superimposes them on what Charles sees and hears in the present (73). Even more disturbingly the letter evokes a wider world that includes Brideshead, the countryside, and Venice: a "there" in which Sebastian is free and into which he has not invited Charles.

Even when he does invite Charles, by means of his alarming telegram, Charles must go through a series of trials before he can return to the "enclosed and enchanted garden" (31) with Sebastian. The second train journey to Brideshead (in narrative time, which in fiction is more important than calendar time) on the "golden evening" (75) contrasts with the one described in the prologue because Charles's fears make the second trip a psychological ordeal. The news of Sebastian's actual condition brings no relief because Charles finds Julia's sex and level of sophistication—though a year younger, she seems far more mature than Charles and Sebastian—as intimidating as her implication that he is a mere adjunct to Sebastian. Ryder uses the image of field glasses, through which one sees another person in detail before realizing "that one is to him a distant speck, doubtfully human" (76), to establish the psychological equivalent of the here/there contrast, which is reinforced by her distancing him by calling him "Mr. Ryder".

Brideshead, the physical goal of his journey, rewards Charles for the rigors of his ordeal and exorcises the dreary atmosphere of his father's house. During this visit, Brideshead is open rather than, as on the first, shuttered and shrouded, and rather than being hustled through it, Charles is welcomed to examine it at leisure. He sits at ease in the painted parlour. As "a single composition, the design of one illustrious hand" at a particular moment in the past (Sebastian's view of it as "cosy" may evoke but does not mention Anthony Blanche's criticism), it dispels the memory of his father's garden room and eclectic antiquarianism. The windows of the Brideshead library, open to the sight of lakes and stars, to pleasant smells, and to the sound of water, contrast directly with the windows to the room in London, which admit neither sights nor smells and contain only "the ticking of the clocks, the distant murmur of traffic on the Bayswater Road, and my father's regular turning of the pages" (65).

This chapter is a bit shorter and far simpler in construction than those in the rest of book 1 because its major function is to dispel the pastoral mood and to prepare for and effect a transition to the intensification and the development of the effects of that mood. Thus the "Dresden figures of pastoral gaiety" (62), which Ryder dismissed at the beginning of the chapter, return as the "prim Pompeian figures . . . in pastoral groups" (77) on the dome of the painted parlour to reestablish the tone of chapter 1 and to prepare for the next chapter. The last sentence of the chapter, suddenly introducing the quintessentially anti-pastoral image of air raid sirens, both reinforces Charles's sense of relief and reestablishes the adult perspective of Ryder in wartime for the last time in book 1. From this point on, chapters depend for their structure less on contrasts in mood and more on the complexity of relationships and their consequences.

CHAPTER 4

Like its predecessor, this chapter is divided into two major sections, and it picks up and develops in considerable detail the attractions of enchanted gardens—Brideshead Castle and Venice—whose inhabitants are protected from complexity and consequences in surroundings of great, and increasing, worldly splendor. But chapter 4 reverses the movement towards simplicity. The two part division is more complex than in chapter 3 because each half is in turn divided into two thematically functional parts. In both halves, the first part establishes a version of the pastoral world, a space ("here" in the terms established by the novel) beautiful in its self-consistent harmony. The second part of each half introduces the element of time before and to come (the novel's "then") and complications of social, psychological, and moral issues that threaten that world. In the second half, the garden is wider and more luxurious than in the first, but the threats to its stability are much more immediate and cannot be answered or ignored.

The movement of the chapter is less rapid and the thematic development is less obtrusive than this outline can indicate. In fact, the pace of the chapter is deliberate, and worldly pleasures and talents are given their full due. Thus the chapter begins with Ryder's meditation on languor (critics with tastes formed by the more austere side of modernist writing may find it too exclamatory, rhetorical in the bad sense) which reinforces emphatically by position and development his approval of his younger self and of the pastoral world. Languor is represented as a stage of development that seems to escape time and process, and an image of eternal states of bliss in limbo or heaven and—the narrative movement implies—a preparation of the individual soul for those states foreshadowed in the passage about the "new truth . . . in whose light all our previous knowledge must be rearranged" (79).

The subjective and atemporal quality of this passage is momentarily disturbed by Sebastian's knowledge that life cannot be like this—"always summer, always alone, the fruit always ripe and Aloysius in a good temper" (79). But the pastoral mood returns in the series of images that concludes with the vision of "Sebastian as he was now" (a beautiful example of the complexities of time, viewpoint, and grammar inherent in retrospective first person narration), and the mood is reinforced by the structure used in the next ten pages. Rather than following chronological sequence, this material is arranged atemporally by topic (art, wine, religion) in order to emphasize the separation from the outer world and to allow Waugh to contrast actor's and writer's levels of awareness. Charles thinks only of the pleasures of sketching and of drinking; Ryder sees the way in which these experiences have shaped and enriched his life.

Although Charles thinks of himself as sequestered (*Webster's New Collegiate Dictionary* lists "secluded" and "withdrawn" as synonyms), he is in fact developing his talents and expanding his view of the world. For example, Sebastian does not care when the dome was built because he reacts instinctively and (Blanche would say) charmingly. Collins, whom Sebastian invokes to try to stop Charles from asking questions, would know all the dates and influences and perceive none of the beauty. But Charles, seeking a mean between the extremes of Sebastian and Collins, desires to know about the dome as well as to feel its effect, and Ryder's account of the terrace, "the final consummation of the house's plan" (80), shows that he has found a happy medium—and foreshadows the final view of the terrace in the epilogue (347).

Charles, dazzled by the variety and elegance of Brideshead, has not reached Ryder's level of understanding, but the process of drawing the fountain forces him to contemplate it, and as a result he feels "a whole new system of nerves alive within me, as though the water that spurted and bubbled among its stones was indeed a life-giving spring" (82), a kind of aesthetic baptism into a whole new realm of art. The effect of his first oil painting is less spectacular, but he does learn something about the medium; he does, in a modest way, give to as well as receive from Brideshead; and he does learn something about his own limitations. For one thing, though Charles may not be conscious of it, he cannot portray people, only objects and landscapes, and he will not be able to paint another person until well into book 2.

Charles's enjoyment of wine is rather like his enjoyment of architecture and painting: naive, playful, and productive. Ryder as connoisseur sees wine as "the seed of that rich harvest which was to be my stay in many barren years" (83), and the combination of knowledge and delight leads, like his painting, to contemplation as well as intoxication.

The third and ultimately most significant topic of this section—

religion—fails to stimulate or even interest Charles at this point. Waugh deliberately introduces the subject by means of the commonplace Fr. Phipps, and throughout the novel he takes pains to characterize priests as ordinary, practical men with a job to do. This is partly due to Waugh's personal taste and partly due to his desire to make religion seem a normal part of life. Charles is slightly more interested in religion than he is in cricket only because of Sebastian, who himself is very far from realizing "that these quaint observances expressed a coherent philosophical system and intransigeant historical claims" (86). Sebastian responds to religion as he does to everything else, concentrating on the "lovely idea" of the Christmas story and the efficiency of St. Anthony of Padua in finding lost objects and skipping from questions of personal morality to newspaper stories of child molestation and abortion without making any connection. He does outline the religious status of each member of his family—a kind of footnote to and modification of Anthony Blanche's characterizations—and notes that "happiness doesn't seem to have much to do with it" (89).

The incursion of Lord Brideshead (he is never given a first name) and Cordelia marks the end of Charles and Sebastian's idyll by introducing both dramatic and thematic complications. Waugh links them with previous action: Bridey's appearance confirms Anthony Blanche's description in chapter 2, and Cordelia's familiar use of "Charles" sets off Julia's stiff and formal "Mr. Ryder" in chapter 3. Although both are "fervent Catholics," Bridey represents the letter and Cordelia the spirit of their religion: Brideshead questions Charles about his agnosticism; Cordelia promises to pray for him. In both, the attitude towards the art nouveau chapel indicates that Catholicism has no more to do with taste than it does with happiness. Still, however stiff and overprecise Bridey may be, he puts both art and wine into a context: as means to an end, not as ends in themselves. Bridey's generalization is very close to the implications of Ryder's remarks about Charles's drawing, which teaches him to see the fountain, and his painting, which teaches him about a new material. Neither is important for what it is, only for where it leads.

The appearance of Bridey and Cordelia also develops the dramatic issue, raised in both chapters 1 and 2, of the effect of Sebastian's family on him and on Charles. Though hardly the "ravening beasts" (79) of Sebastian's fears, they help to show Charles a side of Sebastian that he cannot comprehend and therefore they reveal, though they do not cause, a previously undetected gap between the two friends. As with earlier elements of plot, this is not developed immediately. Instead, it adds another element to the atmosphere—more significant than plot here and in the novel as a whole—in which Charles observes and gradually perceives motives and actions that he cannot control.

In the second half of chapter 4, the trip to Venice, Waugh uses narrative as the major principle of structure. The shift in technique provides a contrast to the languid, lyric mode of the Brideshead sequence; the shift in scene takes Charles and Sebastian into a larger world—a different and stranger "there"—which puts their relationship in new perspectives of time and space; and the introduction of characters to embody new values establishes different moral, social, and psychological contexts.

Like the Brideshead sequence, the Venetian half is constructed in two parts. But instead of beginning with carefully sorted ideas and responses as the first half had done, each part of the second half begins with a myriad of new sensations blurred into a background and then gradually focuses on a single figure.

The long paragraph describing the journey to Venice is unlike Waugh's four earlier travel books and his novels, especially *Black Mischief* and *Scoop,* in which journeys have a major role. In the travel books, odd and amusing characters stand out from the physical and human background; in the novels, discontinuous images reveal the characters' estrangement from their surroundings. But here, in what must be the least uncomfortable third-class train journey in fact or fiction, Waugh emphasizes by the clear division of stages, the heavy use of series in the sentence structure, and the selection or omission of detail the smoothness of the journey, as if to indicate the coherence and essential benevolence of the world through which Charles and Sebastian move. Also, of course, theirs contrasts with other train journeys in the novel, especially that in the prologue.

The palazzo is like a set created to feature Lord Marchmain, who is introduced cinematically, first as a silhouette and voice and then, a page later, as a face in full light. His appearance and way of life confirm Anthony Blanche's earlier description, but more significant and more overt is the contrast that Charles twice makes with his own father, and which is reinforced by the echo of "poppet" (78, 100) from Julia's response to Charles's description of his father. All children make this kind of comparison. Edward Ryder suffers in Charles's view because Lord Marchmain is the kind of man—urbane, rich, handsome, sexually and socially competent—that an adolescent male would like to become. While both fathers play roles, Lord Marchmain's seems far more attractive.

The second part of the Venetian half of the chapter begins rather than ends by describing its dominant figure, Cara, and it does so by analysis rather than by cinematic images. Lord Marchmain looks his Byronic part; Cara acts and looks eminently respectable, confirming Blanche's description of her as "a personable, middle-aged lady" (56). She presides over the two weeks of tourism described in a passage parallel in style and function to the train journey south, but she functions most significantly as moral analyst.

Unlike Bridey, she is interested in particular cases as well as in general principle, and thus she is able to put Charles's love for Sebastian into emotional and temporal perspective, seeing it as good if it is a stage in development—a means—and does not go on too long or become an end in itself. More important, she adds another and very different view of the Marchmains. Lady Marchmain is characterized not as Anthony Blanche's vampire or the smothering parent of Charles's inferences but as "a good and simple woman who has been loved in the wrong way" (103). And Lord Marchmain's Byronic, indifferent pose is questioned. Cara's analysis suggests the real reason why Lord Marchmain is the only member of his family with whom Sebastian willingly associates: neither has grown up, the father "hating all the illusions of boyhood," the son "in love with his own childhood" (103). Both seek to evade the complexity of the adult world in ways that Charles presumably will not.

Charles can find no better response to Cara's benevolence than he could to Blanche's malice, and like the Oxford sequence in chapters 1 and 2, this chapter and the long vacation end anticlimactically. Once again, as in chapter 2, the pastoral mood has been unable to resist the pressures of the outside world. But in chapter 2 the problem lay in estimating a character and situation that Blanche presented as static. Here the situation is dynamic and unstable, and the question is less how Charles will feel than what Sebastian will do.

Chapter 5

This chapter is the first in *Brideshead Revisited* to use dramatic structure as a major principle of organization. It is even possible, with a little trimming here and a little forcing there, to divide the chapter into five parts, like a well-made play: exposition, three increasing levels of complication rising to a climax, and resolution. And Waugh provides internal hints—"a new epoch," "the first step" (both on 129), and Sebastian's "third disaster" (141)—that reinforce the idea of dramatic structure.

Yet it is always a mistake for the writer or the critic to impose a rigid pattern on organic material and create a kind of intellectual bonsai. Chapter 5 is part of a large novelistic structure, not an independent drama, and though on the surface it is organized by movement from one event to the next, it continues, like previous chapters, to use contrast—of characters, settings, and atmospheres—as a major principle of construction. Moreover, the continued presence of Ryder as narrator helps Waugh to modulate from action to reflection and from prospect to retrospect and thereby to emphasize not the forward movement of events but Ryder's understanding of them.

To achieve this end, Waugh begins to use cause and effect as a major structural principle to depict the mutual and disastrous consequences of Lady Marchmain's attempt to create an atmosphere in which to hold Sebastian, Sebastian's attempt to escape, the imposition of tighter limitations, and more frantic and self-destructive flight. As the chapter develops, the here/there, then/now contrasts that dominated the novel up to this point are not so much undermined as dispelled. In the new year and the new mode, "here," with the enchantment gone, is very much like "there," the enclosure a room, even a cell, rather than a garden, a trap rather than a refuge. "Now" becomes "then" in a process that cannot be escaped by returning to the past.

At first, however, atmosphere—autumnal, damp, dimmed—dominates opening paragraphs that pronounce the *vale* (classically educated, Waugh would have used the Latin term for "farewell") to the Arcadian Oxford that Charles and Sebastian had shared and to Cousin Jasper and Anthony Blanche, who had helped to define its limits. The gillyflowers beneath Charles's window (they will reappear at the end of the chapter) are replaced by damp leaves; the sunshine gives way to mist; anarchic pleasure gives way to solid citizenship or morose and solitary binges. Charles discovers that, with Jasper gone, it seems natural to follow his advice and become, "soberly dressed and happily employed . . . a fairly respectable member of my college" (107).

Jasper's spirit is placed before Charles's new way of life to emphasize cause and effect. The *vale* to Anthony Blanche, however, comes after the contrast between Charles and Sebastian, who is compelled "to escape from reality" (107). Like Jasper, Blanche provided a context for the fun; unlike Jasper, his example cannot live after him: departing, "he had locked a door and hung the key on his chain" (107). This stage door is not the "low door in the wall" that led to the "enclosed and enchanted garden" (31) that Charles has entered with Sebastian. Anthony is a stage manager rather than an Arcadian shepherd, but his theater provided Sebastian with a self-contained world of play into which he could escape. The long analogy with the charity matinee emphasizes both compelling quality and the artificial and inverted qualities of Blanche's talents. Like the rest of the group, Charles and Sebastian are left without scenario or direction when he leaves.

If one were to insist on the five-act structure of the chapter, this overture (actually a kind of cloture) could be described as the prologue. In structural terms, it may be connected to the next three pages, but the texture of these two passages is very different. The first dispels the old atmosphere and characters; the second begins to assemble a new, specifically non-Arcadian cast, representatives of the adult world who first protect Sebastian from the consequences of his alcoholism ("enablers" in the terminology of those who deal with substance abuse) and then try to become his keepers.

Both Mr. Samgrass and Rex Mottram embody different kinds of worldly wisdom to the point of parody. Samgrass, a consummate academic politician and careerist, is the first Oxford official to appear onstage: Blanche could escape his anonymous and "p-p-preposterous tutor" (32), but Samgrass is ubiquitous and insidious. Samgrass knows about the illustrious dead; Mottram moves easily, or claims to, among the notorious living—the figures mentioned on page 111 were prominent, respectively, in the highest levels of society, journalism, politics, theater, painting, and boxing. Both Samgrass and Mottram help move the action but are not affected by it. They help to set off and to define each other and, more significantly, Lady Marchmain and Julia, characters who will play larger and more complex roles in the plot and theme of the novel.

At this point Samgrass almost overshadows Lady Marchmain. The third enabler and keeper, she is the most enigmatic if not the most complex character in the novel. In contrast to the elaborate and carefully lighted presentation of her husband, she is introduced almost casually and even then is presented not dramatically but in terms of Charles's response to her and Sebastian's sour though indirect comment echoing his prophecy that his family will usurp Charles's friendship. Waugh chose to introduce Lady Marchmain in this way for at least two reasons. First, he needed to vary the technique of introducing Sebastian's parents. Second, in larger formal terms it was necessary to create a very strong immediate impression of Lord Marchmain, who would not reappear for some two hundred pages, while Lady Marchmain, who will figure prominently throughout this chapter and the next, can be introduced less directly because her significance will almost immediately become apparent (see *Evelyn Waugh, Writer*, 156–62).

The first real action of the chapter—act one in dramatic terms—comes in the trip to London for Rex Mottram's dance. Several elements—most notably the use of the long-suffering and invisible Hardcastle's car and a barely avoided collision, and perhaps the idea of women as dangerous—recall Charles and Sebastian's idyllic trip to Brideshead in chapter 1. Here, however, the destination unknown to Charles is not the nursery and Nanny Hawkins but the Old Hundredth, the whores, and the jail cell. In chapter 1, they avoid Julia as a representative of the family; here they seek her out as an intermediary to Lady Marchmain. Furthermore, in chapter 1 Charles and Sebastian are blissfully alone; here they are accompanied by Boy Mulcaster, whose blustering and false sophistication makes their response to the women more attractive than it might otherwise seem. But for the first time, their actions have real consequences, legal, academic, and domestic, and they need the worldly power of, and are thus indebted to, Samgrass and Mottram. Sebastian's apparently unreasonable desire to avoid his mother's reaction, though subordinated to other concerns, serves as a reminder of her power over him.

In structural terms, the Christmas party at Brideshead constitutes the second act of chapter 5, but in the usual sense the sequence is hardly dramatic. First, Waugh uses Mr. Samgrass to make the transition from the London fiasco through the rest of the fall term at Oxford to the gathering at Brideshead, and while Samgrass's pretensions are amusing, they do little to advance the plot. Like Anthony Blanche, however, he sets a tone, thus reinforcing the contrast between the two Oxfords of summer and autumn. And his attempt to act as stage manager of the Christmas party, introducing the cast of characters, makes Charles seem less of an outsider for his first visit to the Flyte family.

The episode is important primarily because it establishes a pattern for the remaining episodes of the chapter in which Lady Marchmain's talks with Charles alternate with Sebastian's response. In this section, Lady Marchmain talks to Charles, and Sebastian leaves, ostensibly to avoid Samgrass. Both the content and the setting of her conversations about religion reveal something about her intentions, which are lofty, and her taste, which is not. But the major function of the talks is to prepare for the scene ten pages later in which she tries to comprehend Sebastian's drinking.

The "little talks" are followed by the analysis of Sebastian's uneasiness in order to establish the cause-effect relationship between Lady Marchmain's efforts and Sebastian's response; and the extended comparison of Sebastian with the Polynesian turning away from the door to face the wall reinforces the image of Aloysius as abandoned fetish (106) and contrasts with the image of the door into the enchanted garden which has served as the emblem of Charles and Sebastian's youthful Arcadia. The levels of knowledge of character and narrator are different: Ryder understands that Sebastian's prophecy of his family's separating him and Charles is self-fulfilling (though Waugh would resist putting it this way, Sebastian is like a child who cannot have, or allow another to have, more than one friend at a time) and that Sebastian finds intolerable the larger and more complex world of conscience and obligation. Charles catches hints of this, but the action proper makes Samgrass the ostensible antagonist and motivates the flight to Charles's house where Sebastian is surprisingly welcome. Or perhaps—since Edward Ryder is also fleeing from adult complexity—it is not surprising that he likes Sebastian, though on the more obvious level his response further testifies to Sebastian's charm.

The transition to the Easter party, like that to the Christmas party, uses Samgrass to set the tone for months of life at Oxford, but here Waugh subordinates the don's oiliness to Charles's, and Ryder's, growing understanding of Sebastian's deterioration. The episode that follows reverses the pattern of its predecessor: first Sebastian acts; then his family reacts in an ascending sequence of concern and of knowledge— Julia, Cordelia, Brideshead, Lady Marchmain. Sebastian's flight to London, an overt rejection of his family, forces his mother to abandon charming statements for anguished questions and requires Charles to choose between "the august, masculine atmosphere of a better age" represented by the castle of Lord Marchmain's family and the sitting room emblematic of "the intimate feminine, modern world" (138) and the religion presented within it. This option seems to confine rather than offer Arcadian freedom, and Charles closes its door behind him without regret.

At Christmas Samgrass had come to Brideshead to begin work on a book. At Easter, the volume is Lady Marchmain's farewell gift to Charles. Unable to distinguish between her faith and her feminine charm (127), he is able to dismiss both, but both Charles and Ryder are attracted to the stern masculine heritage and chivalric spirit destroyed in the First World War. Ryder can lament the fact that "These men must die to make a world for Hooper" (139) in a class-conscious version of a widespread attitude toward World War I,[32] but there is little sign that he attempts to emulate them and some evidence that Lady Marchmain's expectations, based on her private cult, are helping to destroy Sebastian.

The final sequence, which closes Charles's and Sebastian's Oxford careers, combines the patterns of the Christmas and Easter parties: Lady Marchmain has a "little talk" with Charles; Sebastian drinks to escape her control; Lady Marchmain expresses her grief at his action and—a further development—dismisses Charles as an unsatisfactory source of information about and tether for her son. In dramatic terms, the climax of the chapter comes in Sebastian's "third disaster" (141), which results in his being "sent down" or suspended.

The rest of the chapter can be seen as an epilogue in which Charles takes leave of the Oxford represented by Collins in a scene where communication, though refused, is at least possible; of his father in a dialogue in which purpose precludes feeling; and of Lady Marchmain in a letter to which no response is thinkable. Turned out of the enchanted garden and half-willingly cutting himself off from his past, Charles turns to a new career and reluctantly enters adult life.

9

The Barren Years

In the 1960 edition, Waugh shifted chapters six through eight of the first edition's book 1 to form book 2, "Brideshead Deserted." This was his final attempt to solve a major structural problem: modulating from pastoral to wasteland in theme and tone and from one major period of action to the next. In dramatic terms, these three chapters are not very effective because they show characters retreating rather than advancing, but they create the sense of hiatus necessary for the action to resume after the ten-year gap that separates the two books of the first edition.

CHAPTER 6

This chapter has many features in common with the Christmas and Easter sequences of chapter 5: Samgrass is chorus and foil; members of the family react, in sequence and in ensemble, to Sebastian's drinking; Lady Marchmain has a little talk with Charles; Charles abandons a place where he has been happy; news from that place follows him. But in chapter 5 the characters react to new situations; in chapter 6 they must deal with repetitions of Sebastian's alcoholic behavior which are like "A blow, expected, repeated, falling on a bruise, with no smart or shock of surprise, only a dull and sickening pain and the doubt whether another like it could be borne" (167). As a result, chapter 6 is undramatic, if drama is defined narrowly as relying on anticipation and suspense. Instead, this chapter reveals what has already happened or can only be repeated. Moreover, as Charles begins to live independently of Brideshead and Sebastian, "here" and "there," "then" and "now" become more widely separated in space and time. Charles begins to move from the Arcadian garden to the modern world, and for the first time since chapter 3 Ryder begins to refer to experiences that come between narrated past and narrating present. Furthermore, Waugh begins to close the gap between them in a process that will occupy the rest of the novel.

At the beginning of the chapter, Waugh signals the shift in purpose by a shift in narrative strategy. Instead of devoting a paragraph or more to transitions, as in the first five chapters, he begins in the middle of Samgrass's travelogue. The usual elements of exposition—setting, time, appearance of characters—are deferred for two full pages, perhaps to imply that the characters themselves wish to ignore elements that measure change.

More obviously, Samgrass becomes, as he had the previous Christmas, a kind of scapegoat upon whom the members of the family displace their uneasiness with one another. Here the tactic does not work because Sebastian, in "the shadows beyond the lamp-light, beyond the warmth of the burning logs, beyond the family circle and the photographs spread out on the card-table" (149), is no longer willing to play that or any other family game. And his isolation gives the signal less of action to come—the attempts to keep alcohol from Sebastian provide the narrative structure but do not carry the real point of the chapter—than of past action to be revealed.

The first expository material, which summarizes Charles's and Sebastian's simultaneous arrival at Brideshead, reinforces the impression that Samgrass is withholding the truth, and the impression is further reinforced on the return to the narrated present, as Sammy goes for the "little talk" with Lady Marchmain in which he must avoid coming to the point. At the same time, Sebastian visits Nanny Hawkins, but here the nursery cannot serve as magical refuge from his genetic mother. Instead, the familiar surroundings measure the degrees of Sebastian's deterioration in appearance and manner. Because Charles does not wish to deal with the consequences of these changes, he talks of his own activities in the months during which, separated from Sebastian, he has begun to live his own life as an art student in Paris, a "there" which, in a major shift in attitude, is preferable to "here" at Brideshead. Sebastian's corresponding and more extensive story of his activities accounts for the changes in him that Charles has observed and prepares, though preparation is by this time hardly necessary, for the behavior that follows.

Extensive preparation is not required because, as Lady Marchmain observes in a slightly different context, everyone has "been through it all before" (137). Sebastian's joining the fox hunt produces general euphoria not simply because, as his mother thinks, he is following aristocratic tradition but because, as no one says, the last time he seemed really normal at Brideshead was the hunt in chapter 5. The conversations about Sebastian—Julia dismissive and self-centered, Bridey sober and theological, Lady Marchmain distracted and accusatory—echo in subject and tone the corresponding scenes in chapter 5.

Waugh does vary the presentation of Sebastian's drunk scenes. Like a well-constructed horror movie, the chapter confounds expectation, so that when the audience expects the worst, nothing happens, and when they relax, bang goes the door and the monster erupts. Of course, Waugh is presenting a menace more familiar than a carnivorous vegetable from outer space or a deranged and omnipresent handyman, and he lets the reading audience know what is going to happen. But he does play with the family's expectation that Sebastian will appear drunk and then with their belief that he will appear sober. He does so not just to vary the action but to reveal the insecurity of living with an alcoholic.[33] The metaphor of fire in a ship's hold (163)— unseen, pervasive, destructive—concentrates and emphasizes the family's emotional response. All of the characters in chapter 6 reach a new level of awareness: the family realizes their helplessness; Sebastian his immediate alternatives; and Charles the futility of trying to help Sebastian and of choosing sides in a conflict that no one can win.

Because of the pain that Sebastian's behavior causes, Waugh overtly attempts to clear Charles of Lady Marchmain's charges that, in giving Sebastian money, he has been "callously wicked" or "wantonly cruel" (168). Charles refuses Sebastian's first request; he grants it only when he is convinced that Lady Marchmain has changed her tactics from manipulation to coercion. He thinks coercion futile; he knows that it is distasteful; and, forced to choose between mother and son, he chooses Sebastian. Perhaps more important, the subsequent revelation that Cordelia has followed his example implies that he has been motivated by compassion for his friend because Cordelia is, as the Latin root of her name implies, the heart and thus the emotional center of the family.

The epilogue to chapter 6 is longer than the corresponding section in chapter 5 for several reasons. Structurally, Waugh has to establish Charles very firmly in his new career because Charles will disappear for just over twenty pages while Ryder catches up with Julia's activities. Dramatically, the epilogue deals not only with Charles moving out of the picture but also with Rex Mottram moving in. Emotionally, Charles must bid farewell to the illusions of youth and find an alternative to the pastoral world he shared with Sebastian. (In *Scoop* Waugh had previously used images of the undersea world, perhaps drawing from the closing lines of T. S. Eliot's "The Love Song of J. Alfred Prufrock," to create a similar suggestion of an amoral, sensual world outside the bounds of normal experience.)[34] Because that vision has failed, he thinks it delusory and turns away from charm to a world measurable by the senses.

Even in that world, in which Charles is aware that "I was leaving part of myself behind" (169), it is possible and even necessary to make discriminations, and that is the purpose of the scenes with Rex Mottram with which the chapter concludes. Critics have been particularly severe in pointing to the restaurant scene as an indication of Ryder's, and Waugh's, snobbery in exulting over Mottram's ignorance,[35] and as I noted earlier, Waugh himself came to regard the book as "infused with a kind of gluttony, for food and wine" and less tangible elements, "which now with a full stomach I find distasteful" (*Brideshead*, 1960, 9).

To attack Ryder and Waugh, critics have to defend Mottram, whose every quality and habit are ordinarily despised by literary intellectuals everywhere in the world. One might conclude that they suspect that Waugh would have regarded them—especially the Americans—in the same way. (They would be wrong to do so; Waugh thought academics funny and was willing to fight critics on equal, if not equitable, terms.) Whatever their motivation, critics miss an important point: Rex is not merely ignorant; he is pretentious. Furthermore, his lack of taste in, and for, food and wine results from his adopting secondhand opinions rather than acquiring real taste. His lighting a cigarette between courses is the grossest but not the only sign of his failure to pay the tribute of real attention to a superb meal. And this defect in taste indicates a moral defect because he treats people the way he treats food and drink. He knows what he has been told, and he can read labels, but he will not even try to taste the difference between the fine recent brandy and the pseudo-Napoleonic syrup; he makes no distinction between Julia and any other debutante of aristocratic lineage who could play the role of "leading young political hostess" (177); and he is consistently callous about the emotional, physical, and financial problems of the family he intends to join.

Because he is a perfectly awful man, one could ask why Charles consents to dine with him. In terms of character, the answer is twofold: Charles is curious about what the Flytes have said of him and he feels a sense of obligation towards the man who extracted him from jail. In terms of structure, the answer is more complex. Perhaps Waugh desired to give a relatively objective presentation of Rex in action before the next chapter's perspective on him in the entirely ungrateful role of a lover's ex-husband. Perhaps his callousness about the Flytes' current and impending misfortunes is a way of indicating Charles's growing distance from the family. Almost certainly—though, as I have indicated, Waugh did not succeed with all critics—Rex's blunt, man-of-the-world realism is intended to provide a contrast with Charles's perspective as he gets closer to becoming the apparently cynical and disillusioned Ryder.

It is for that reason, perhaps, that Waugh resumes the technique of creating temporal perspective in the contrast between the odd and luxurious bathroom at Brideshead and "the uniform, clinical little chambers . . . which pass for luxury in the modern world" (153–54); later, he has Ryder find continuity between the burgundy he drank with Rex and a bottle of the same vintage tasted fourteen years later, "in the first autumn of the war," which indicates to Ryder "that mankind in its long passion had learned [a] wisdom" other than Rex's (175). That wisdom seems to view the product of human skill, change though it may, as a sign of secular grace, missing from Mottram's "harsh, acquisitive world" (175–76). Charles may have left behind the part of himself that found wisdom in knowing and loving another human being, but Rex has never found or even suspected this part of himself. Charles can mourn the loss of Brideshead; Rex, well on his way to acquiring one of its prizes, has no standards by which to value it.

Chapter 7

We may condemn for lack of foresight someone in the classical farcical situation of painting himself into a corner, but the exercise of moral superiority is less interesting and certainly less instructive than watching someone try to get out of his predicament as quickly and as cleanly as possible. Chapter 7 is Waugh's corner. In it he has to deal with a problem inherent in all novels in which first person narrators tell other people's stories: how to incorporate material that the narrator has not personally experienced.

When an otherwise competent artist seems to make a mistake, the critic should pause before condemning. Sometimes it *is* a mistake, but it is rarely just a mistake. Given the ingenuity with which the rest of the novel is constructed, it seems impossible that Waugh did not recognize in advance this chapter's problems: interrupting the momentum of the narrative, effacing Charles, and depending upon summary interspersed with awkward reminders that material is reported second hand. On the other hand, the chapter does some things that need doing: it establishes Julia more firmly as a counterpart to Sebastian; it reveals the motives for her interest in and marriage to Rex; it traces her alienation from her religion and her family; it accounts for the contrast between Rex's ambitious plans for marriage to Julia and their inglorious fulfillment, both developed at the end of chapter 6; it continues the process of decline in Lady Marchmain's physical health and moral control; and it fills the gap in dramatic time (after February 1925) and narrative time (after May 1925) between the end of chapter 6 and the beginning (in May 1926) of chapter 8.

Primarily, of course, the chapter is intended to prepare the reader for the prominence that Julia will assume in book 2 of the novel and to create the emotional context in which Ryder sees her. Waugh knew he was undertaking a difficult characterization, as distinct from construction. In *Work Suspended* the narrator, a professional novelist, poses the question: "To write of someone loved, of oneself loving, above all of oneself being loved—how can these things be done with propriety? How can they be done at all?" (*Work Suspended*, 81). The answer most critics have given about Julia is, "Not very well," and the relative flatness of Julia in the Granada television production cannot be blamed on scriptwriter, director, or actress. Waugh had greater success in creating strong, even ruthless, and amoral women characters, all the way from Margot Beste-Chetwynde in *Decline and Fall* at the beginning of his career through Virginia Troy in *The End of the Battle* at its conclusion, than he did in creating virtuous women.[36]

In presenting Julia, Waugh seems to have made a mistake that he had avoided in the case of Sebastian: attempting to dazzle the audience with her glamor before presenting her thoughts and actions. In chapter 1, Sebastian is shown to be attractive because he is introduced in glorious surroundings doing very pleasant things, and Charles's bemusement with him is understandable. The beginning of chapter 7 is so little scenic that we are never sure when or how Ryder got the information he passes on. It is certain that neither Charles nor Ryder witnesses the scenes of Julia's debutante triumphs and the summary of—more a speculation about—the spectators' response to her as bluebird or kingfisher seems forced and unconvincing. Waugh does use Julia's first encounter with Charles in chapter 3 as a kind of framing device for Julia's debut (179, 180, 183), but because the meeting showed that they had nothing in common, this device is more like temporary scaffolding than structural beams.

When, however, Ryder begins to analyze Julia's response to her situation and to reveal her doubts, inexperience, and snobbery, she seems more believable and even more attractive than she did as top debutante. The images of the magic ring that calls the subservient monster—the figure governing the presentation of Rex for much of the chapter—and of her plans for marriage as a military map work better than the image of the kingfisher first because they are analytic rather than sentimental and second because they reveal something about her character, her powers of self-analysis, and her future.

At this point, she regards marriage as a mere tactical move in a larger social strategy, and she constructs her fantasy husband according to what possessions he has and what inconvenient qualities, such as intelligence, passion, and will, he does not have. "Eustace," as she calls this fantasy figure, is very useful in explaining Julia's interest in Rex Mottram. Eustace is tied to the past—a country house, a solid position, a deceased wife—and would provide a ready-made setting for Julia. Rex thrusts into the future with all of his considerable powers of will, strength, and concentration. Bored with or threatened by the various little worlds she knows, Julia chooses him because at some level she wants to move in his larger world. Eustace would have bought her engagement ring at Cartier's; Rex gets a much more striking ring custom-designed at wholesale price. But unlike Julia, who is Rex's "Eustace," Rex cannot get beyond mere tactics or jockeying for advantage.

Julia is also impressed, and troubled, by the physical sexuality to which she responds with excitement and guilt. Before 1965 or so, "made love" (186) referred to rather more limited activities— passionate kissing and above-the-waist fondling (see page 198 for further evidence)—than what is now implied, but Catholics of that period were taught that these actions or even imagining these actions was mortally sinful. Sex was to be reserved for marriage—except for the carefully restricted expressions of affection engaged couples were allowed (188). Obviously this teaching put a good deal of strain on relationships, real and fictional, and Julia ceases to practice her religion.

In contrast, Rex tries to become a Catholic, but his attitude toward religion is much like his attitude toward food and wine: he can remember what he is told, but he is entirely incapable of discriminating between good and bad advice. He can think only in terms of immediate tactical advantage: as a Catholic, he can be married in a cathedral filled with cardinals hired for the occasion (rather like a movie set with extras from central casting) and thus establish a firmer social base. He really is invincibly ignorant, in ways different from the Protestant girls of Julia's imagination (181) because he lacks the capacity for spiritual perception.

His credulity seems funny when Cordelia exploits it, but even here it is symptomatic of a bottomless ignorance not only of individual laws of the church but of the whole point of religion, which in theory should not leave "time for anything else" (196) but pervade the whole of life. He might sign up, but he could not in any real sense be "converted" because, as Julia observes, "He wasn't a complete human being at all" but "A tiny bit of a man pretending he was the whole" (200).

Rex is not a complete human being because he has no relationship to his past. In social and dynastic terms, it is bad enough that, as Waugh emphasizes repeatedly, no one knows anything about his background. Lady Marchmain's concern may be snobbish, but it masks the more fundamental desire to know where he comes from psychologically as well as literally. Otherwise one cannot know anything about his social or family ties or what, to extend that metaphor, will bind him. Furthermore, if one is, like Lady Marchmain, concerned about the future as well as the past, genetic concerns are by no means irrelevant. But much more important than any of these concerns is the fact that, for Rex, even his own past simply does not exist. He is genuinely surprised at the Flytes' attitude toward his previous marriage just as, two chapters later (257), he is surprised that Julia resents the continuation of his affair with Brenda Champion. The fact that he cannot see is more important than what he does not see.

By the end of the chapter, Julia has learned to see and is telling her own story from the vantage point of ten years after the event. This change in technique serves two purposes: it anticipates and thus helps to bridge the gap of ten years between books 1 and 2; and it gives formal embodiment to the process of Julia's maturing from mere symbol to mature human being. Furthermore, her retrospective account of her errors serves as a parallel to and an anticipation of Charles maturing into Ryder. Finally, in the larger strategy of the novel, the comments on Rex's partial humanity recall Charles's view that he has left part of himself behind and indicate the possibility that he can recover those parts and be a complete human being.

CHAPTER 8

This chapter must serve so many functions that it may seem to have no clear shape of its own. In narrative terms, it brings the major characters up to date and reestablishes Charles as the lens through which the action is seen. In formal terms, it concludes a major segment of the novel. In thematic terms, it restores and reinforces the here/there, then/now pattern that is subordinated in chapter 7. Chapter 8 is divided into three distinct segments: the General Strike, the mission to Sebastian in Fez, and Charles's paintings of Marchmain House. The unifying principle, less obvious than in earlier chapters, can be discovered only when the process has been completed.

The one-sentence paragraph that begins the chapter defines "now" in precise chronological and historical terms: the General Strike of May 1926. The strike may seem little more than a convenient excuse to bring Charles back to England, and certainly Ryder does not take it seriously, but Charles and many Englishmen, including the youthful Waugh, took it very seriously indeed. Waugh wrote in his diary that after years of casual conversation about coming revolution, he had become aware of

> the fact that there is probably to be a general coal strike at the end of the month and the hope that its consequences are incalculable. And I have begun to think whether perhaps April 1926 may not in time rank with July 1914 for the staging of house parties in socio-logical novels. I suppose that the desire to merge one's individual destiny in forces outside oneself, which seems to me deeply rooted in most people and shows itself in social service and mysticism and in some manner in debauchery, is really only a consciousness that this is already the real mechanism of life which requires so much concen-tration to perceive that one wishes to objectify it in more immediate (and themselves subordinate) forces. (250–51)

Not quite twenty years later, Waugh incorporated these ideas into this chapter. The now at the beginning of chapter 8 is not personal and subjective but social and historical, the first since his mother's death in the war to impinge upon Charles's consciousness. In fact, Waugh makes it clear that Charles returns from Paris in order to enter history, to validate what had been the vicarious experience of other nations' revolutions, other generations' wars.

Instead of a whole new spirit, Charles encounters Anthony Blanche and Boy Mulcaster, figures from his past who, themselves relatively unchanged, help to measure the distance from the "then" of less than two years earlier. Blanche's account of Sebastian, entirely anecdotal, ignores causes and effects of his dissipation. In chapter 2 his monologue disturbed and confused Charles by presenting an alterna-tive view of Sebastian. Here Charles seems unmoved. Instead, Charles takes up with Mulcaster—who fulfills Blanche's prediction that he and his set will talk about putting Blanche in the fountain—and accompa-nies him to various nightclubs, which grant Mulcaster "his simple ambition of being known and liked in such places" (205). Inflamed by drink and patriotism, Charles and Mulcaster desire to "show the dead chaps we can fight too" (205), and this is not just the fighting stage of drink but an impulse, even a compulsion, characteristic of a generation too young to fight in "the war to end all wars," a little guilty about not having fought, and anxious to prove their manhood.[37] Or, in the broader terms Waugh himself had used, "to merge one's individual destiny in forces outside oneself."

Nothing much came of the fictional or the historical strike, but the world that Charles returns to has no place, no "here", for him. In historical terms, the strike indicates a sociopolitical shift: Rex, the new breed of politician, acquires publicity and therefore new power during the strike; Bridey, the heir to power in a feudal conception of society based on ordered and traditional relationships among the classes, cannot find a just cause in the new world, does not participate, and becomes even less relevant politically. In formal terms, the preparations for and the aftermath of the strike anticipate the preparations for the coming war in the final chapter of book 2 as well as the dispersal of the Flytes and the destruction of their home in the epilogue.

The second section of the chapter turns from public history to private destiny. Process, if not history in the usual sense, has overtaken the Flyte family: Julia has a new "gentleness and gravity" (207); her mother is dying; Sebastian is reported to be "in a very bad way" (208). Charles's trip to Fez tests Blanche's report. As in chapter 2, Blanche's account is not inaccurate, but it does not give the full story. Blanche cannot perceive that Sebastian has attempted to re-create, in Fez and with Kurt, the Arcadia he inhabited at Oxford with Charles and from which he has been exiled. The British Consul, a more charitable version of Cousin Jasper and Collins, gives the conventional view of Sebastian as remittance man (paid an allowance to remove an embarrassment from England) and source of anxiety. This is the social, daylight view, "suburban and up-to-date" (210), of Morocco and of Sebastian, but at night, in the walled old city, Charles finds another spirit—an echo of the "enclosed and enchanted garden . . . not overlooked by any window, in the heart of that grey city" of Oxford (31).

Like Sebastian, Kurt has found a replacement for a friend of university days. Charles dislikes Kurt not merely because by any standard he knows, Kurt is impossible but also because Kurt, in parodying Charles, shows him that he is isolated, excluded even from the dim reflection of Arcadia in "the little enclosed house at the end of the alley" (216), apparently a dead end rather than a whole separate world. Charles has, then, neither "here" nor "then" to console and support him. In another sense, Kurt replaces Aloysius the teddy bear in allowing Sebastian to take a parental role. Sebastian calls attention to his need to look after someone else in a comment that Ryder calls "the key I lacked" (215). Sebastian has not been allowed to, perhaps cannot, function in the adult world, but he needs to be a subject rather than an object in the grammar of charity in the full theological sense. And as the contrast between the doctor and the Franciscan brother indicates, Sebastian is not merely a textbook case of alcoholism but an individual soul capable of virtue. Charles leaves with the view that "there was nothing more I could do for Sebastian" (216), implying not only that his relationship with Sebastian is ended but also that Sebastian is fixed in place, removed from the process of action with a finality which Lord Brideshead's logic—Sebastian is unfortunate but competent and must be allowed to live as he wishes—helps to seal.

The third section of the chapter concludes the process of narrowing, moving from public action to personal affection to the exercise of individual talent. Charles's mastery of his art seems to give him an alternative to public action and to love. At this point, he does not realize that his best work is done for and in the literal company of the Flytes, and by the end of the chapter he thinks his work is an end in itself and considers himself a creator from the humanistic and irreligious Renaissance filtered through the Victorian perspective of Robert Browning's poems. He is very full of himself while he believes that he has transcended himself.

The conversation with Cordelia establishes other perspectives. Most fully established dramatically are the change and decay implied in the Latin quotation that translates "How the city sits solitary [that was full of people]" (220) and made explicit by the death of Lady Marchmain, the closing of the chapel at Brideshead, the impending destruction of Marchmain House, and the apostasy from Catholic faith of Lord Marchmain, Julia, and Sebastian.

The other perspective is that of Catholicism, and Cordelia makes the important distinction between true faith and the religion—pious, charming, flirtatious—represented by her mother. Waugh agreed with his agent that "Lady Marchmain is an enigma" and "hoped the last conversation with Cordelia gave the theological clue" (*Letters*, 185), but he did not explain further. He did answer Nancy Mitford's question with "no I am not on her side; but God is, who suffers fools gladly, and the book is about God" (*Letters*, 196). Lady Marchmain is neither, or not merely, the "good and simple woman who has been loved in the wrong way" (103) of Cara's inference, nor simply the "femme fatale" of Sebastian's premature epitaph (214), nor the manipulative and rather saccharine mother of Charles's experience. As Cordelia says, she is saintly—with all the external marks of piety— without having the heroic virtue requisite for sainthood. And because Cordelia more than any other member of her family has sense, including a sense of humor, affection as well as a clearer and more humane faith, she is most suited to analyze her mother. Because Cordelia, unlike Rex, has a lively appetite for food and company, she is a suitable companion for Charles in the expansive secular mood that focuses on the pleasures of the present moment. Because she has the most to lose from the fulfillment of Rex Mottram's predictions of "mortal illness and debt" (175) and yet can remain objective about the temporal situation and hopeful about the spiritual, she can bring to a close this phase of the family's story while allowing, in fact insisting upon, the possibility of a different kind of future in a religious spirit very different from her father's pomposity about "the faith of their ancestors" and her mother's rather frilly piety.

This scene and this chapter conclude the phase of the novel that in 1960 Waugh titled "Brideshead Deserted." The hideous chapel is empty; the London house is about to be destroyed; the Flyte family is dispersed. Meanwhile Charles seems quite content to view all of this entirely in the perspective of his talent.

10

Finding a Home

Whatever principle of division Waugh employed in creating the external structure of *Brideshead Revisited* (see chapter 5 of this book), "A Twitch upon the Thread" was always intended to conclude the framed action and reveal the true purpose of the novel and the characters. The five chapters of book 2 in fact mirror the construction of book 1, for the structure is reversed to begin not in splendor but in barrenness and end not with images of futility (though both end with death and dispersal) but with images of hope (not just secular expectation) that, like the accompanying virtues of faith and charity, can lead to renewal and salvation.

CHAPTER 1

Waugh's most obvious difficulty in the first chapter was the problem of the ten-year gap in time and the more serious interruption in the momentum of the novel. His diaries and letters do not treat the problems directly, but he did concoct for his agent an elaborate plan to revise and publish what he had already written and to delay publishing, and therefore writing, the final section. His agent, A. D. Peters, replied calmly and implacably that among all the other arguments against this transparent evasion, the prologue-body-epilogue structure would then make no sense at all (see *Letters*, 182, and *Evelyn Waugh, Writer*, 121). Driven back to the desk, Waugh persevered, but after finishing a manuscript draft of the first chapter he called it "the most difficult part of the book so far" and worried that "in spite of some passages of beauty I am not sure of my success" (*Diaries*, 564).

His doubts may have come from his awareness that the chapter had to perform a number of formal, dramatic, and narrative tasks that, if not incompatible, were very difficult to unify into a whole. First, of course, he had to begin a major new section that not only establishes continuity with previous material but creates a new tone and new rhythm to govern what is to come. Second, because Ryder as overt narrative voice is subordinated to developing action in the final chapters of book 1, Waugh had not only to reestablish that voice but to indicate a different kind of relationship between narrator and actor as the chronological gap closed. Third, and for immediate purposes most difficult, he had to make palatable as well as plausible Charles's movement away from his wife toward Julia. Finally, or rather simultaneously, he had to continue the process of redefining the here/there, then/now contrasts central to the form of the novel.

The opening paragraphs of chapter 1 (the third and fourth paragraphs of the American edition do not appear in the 1960 edition) may seem to contain digressions, but they work fairly directly to solve the problems inherent in the novel's structure. The short first paragraph, which Waugh revised at least five times (*Evelyn Waugh, Writer*, 148), reestablishes the perspective of Ryder in wartime as a kind of support to hold up the middle between the distant ends of prologue and epilogue. The paragraphs that follow develop the central theme of the value of memory not only for its consoling content but also for its indications that the life of fully human beings can move beyond or above process to illumination and understanding.

As Ryder puts it in simplest terms, "memories are the memorials *and pledges* of the vital hours of a lifetime" (225). Some critics, missing the implications of the words I have italicized, regard the novel as an exercise in self-indulgent nostalgia. At least in intention, Waugh sees memory as connected with artistic inspiration and, by implications realized if not overtly stated in the epilogue, as a sign of God's grace and therefore as an indication of hope for the future.

This concept of memory is extremely important in defining life as more than what happens to a person and for that matter in defining what a person is. The various "counterfeits" (226) accompany and at times submerge the real person, but they are, in the philosophical sense, accidental rather than essential to that person. In these terms, the contrasts between "here" and "there," "then" and "now," defined by space and time, become less significant because they are not determining factors but elements in a pattern.

At least as important as thematic content in the long overture to the chapter and to the book it begins is the new impression it creates of Ryder. For the first time in the novel he speaks at length, not merely in his own voice but from his own mind. This is extremely important because this voice helps Waugh to establish a distinction between Ryder and the Charles of the 1930s that is sharper than that between Ryder and the Charles of the 1920s. In general, the less Charles knows and the less he acts on that knowledge, the less offensive are his errors in behavior and judgment. Thus, at Oxford and Brideshead his enthusiasm tends to excuse his naivete. When he thinks he has the key to life, as in the closing chapters of Book 1, he is more assertive and less pleasant. For most of book 2, he is absolutely certain that his views and actions are correct, and he is, and is intended to be, thoroughly if not absolutely obnoxious.

However, as I argued in chapter 6, this Charles is not Ryder—he is even less Ryder than the Charles of book 1. To sharpen this distinction, Waugh begins book 2 by making Ryder seem more reflective, more tolerant, and more serious than ever before. His attitude towards his former self is one sign of this change. Ryder had excused, even supported, Charles's youthful mistakes, in part because the youth sought to move outside himself to complete that self. But as Ryder implies in the list of counterfeits and states overtly in the judgment of himself as "a small part of myself pretending to be whole" (229), the Charles of the "dead ten years" (256) has become, like Rex Mottram (200), less than human.

As a result, Charles is, as Ryder makes clear, a competent rather than an inspired painter. Waugh told Nancy Mitford that Charles "was a bad painter. Well he was as bad at painting as Osbert [Sitwell] is at writing" (*Letters*, 196), presumably because both had "technical skill, enthusiasm for [their] subject and independence of popular notions" (227). In larger thematic terms, Charles is caught in the "then" and "there," reproducing images from England's cultural past without reinterpreting them, in a style that had become merely nostalgic and decorative rather than structural and organic. The criticism of his work (229) is full of hideously mixed metaphors, but the confusion comes from the work as well as the critic's mind. And the relationships between "here" and "there," "then" and "now," are therefore negative, lacking the necessary life-giving connections, or meaningless, as when Charles refers to the destruction of Anchorage House as "just another jungle closing in" (232).

Charles is a merely fashionable rather than a truly successful painter because he has failed to become a complete human being. That failure is represented in personal terms by his marriage to and relationship with his wife Celia. Her unimportance in the general scheme of things is revealed by the way she is introduced; we learn only tangentially, five pages into the chapter, that Charles has a wife, and her identity is revealed, parenthetically, three pages after that.

Celia has the ungrateful job of representing "here" and "now" to Charles and to the reader. Though prettier and more charming than Rex Mottram, she has thoroughly mastered the material symbols of success in the modern world: she is an inveterate name-dropper and she has no real sense of taste. Both are, in the standards established in the novel, thoroughly appalling. Her conversation, her appearance down to her jewelry, her cocktail party, her reaction to seasickness—all are intended to render her "peculiar charm" (234) unappealing.

Charles's reasons for marrying anyone ("Physical attraction. Ambition. Everyone agrees she's the ideal wife for a painter. Loneliness, missing Sebastian" [257]), and the sister of the appalling Mulcaster at that, indicate the degree of his decline. Her shortcomings, including the infidelity that produced the daughter who carries Charles's name, explain but do not excuse his treatment of her during the scene that presents their reunion and reveal but do not explain her acceptance of this kind of relationship.

One source of difficulty in this sequence has less to do with Waugh's talent than with the sexual mores, or rather the conventions of representing those mores, in the middle 1940s. Waugh's only specific complaint about the difficulty of writing this chapter was on this issue: "I feel very much the futility of describing sexual emotions without describing the sexual act; I should like to give as much detail as I have of the meals, to the two coitions—with his wife and Julia. It would be no more or less obscene than to leave them to the reader's imagination, which in this case cannot be as acute as mine" (*Diaries*, 564–65). Readers of the American edition and of all English editions before 1960 will quite properly wonder about the first coition. Up through page proof and again in the 1960 edition it is quite clear that, after a two-year separation, Celia's "bare back" (230) leads to more than polite conversation, and her "neat, hygienic ways for that too" (*Brideshead*, 1960, 256) prepare a contrast for the highly charged romantic and emotional encounter with Julia.

As Waugh told his wife, he had removed from the novel everything that had upset Fr. Martin d'Arcy, S. J., who had received him into the Catholic church in 1930 (*Letters*, 196). But he may also have wanted to keep from shocking unworldly readers who would turn entirely against Charles. More worldly readers, familiar with conventions of sex between the lines of a novel or scenes of a movie, could infer from the bare back and from the significant gap between Charles turning "back towards his wife" and Celia's beginning to talk again (233, lines 24–25) that something had taken place.

The real point is that for Celia, and at this point for Charles, sex is merely physical, no more satisfying as communication than the dialogue on page 231 in which she does not even suspect that his replies have overtones. Like the modern world that she inhabits, Celia is tone-deaf to nuances: friends are people whose names she recognizes, who send her odorless flowers in cellophane packages, and who can give her some advantage. Her cocktail party, its guests parodied by the little man who crashes it, is properly set on the liner, a "here," as consecutive sentences emphasize, "where wealth is no longer gorgeous and power has no dignity" (237).

Even at this point in his spiritual deadness Charles recalls the phrase "*Quomodo sedet sola civitas*," which Cordelia taught him and which puts the awful modern world into a spiritual context. This is the first link with the personal past before the "dead ten years," and it introduces Julia, a more powerful and much more complex link to that past and hope for a future. It is not merely that Julia reminds him of Sebastian, who becomes the "forerunner" (257) in the pattern of spiritual ascent I discussed in chapter 5, but that she begins the process of changing the values embodied in the contrasts between here and there, then and now.

Thus, though Celia is connected with "here" and "now," Julia is not simply an embodiment of "there" and "then"; the pace and texture of the scenes involving the two women are more significant than any schematic contrasts. Julia has changed (as, Waugh emphasizes on two occasions, Celia has not), and for the first time in the novel change, from Julia as spidery teenager to Julia as mature woman, is presented in positive terms. Perhaps more important, the military, spatial metaphor of no man's land is first established as the norm for interrupted acquaintance and then rejected (238): Julia and Charles are not on the same side of the barbed wire (as Sebastian and Charles were together in the versions of the enchanted garden)—there is no wire and there are no barriers. Space and time have been replaced by less measurable values. Moreover, the erotic element of the affair, both in Charles's disturbed night (250) and in their first night together, is subordinated to his sense of its meaning. The real climax of the chapter occurs in the communication emphasized by the one-sentence paragraph that begins and ends with "I knew what she meant" (253).

Of course, the affair begins during a physical voyage from the new world to the old, and the storm creates and defines an interlude and serves as an emotional (and a natural, as opposed to Celia's artificial settings) backdrop for the beginning of Charles and Julia's romance. The figurative voyage to a new emotional state is also a real voyage, at the end of which the characters will have to deal with customs in all senses of that term. The "orphans of the storm," as Julia calls the pair in an allusion to D. W. Griffith's classic silent film, cannot live in romantic isolation any more than Charles and Sebastian could remain in Arcadia. The immediate dramatic issue is whether Charles and Julia's special timeless place can be integrated into the larger world.

CHAPTER 2

In constructing this chapter, Waugh uses a variation of the structure of book 1, chapter 3. Both are divided by a train journey from London to Brideshead in which the silverware jiggles in the same way and during which the same drink, gin and vermouth, is served (74, 274). In both, Charles is trapped in an oppressive "here" and "now" in London and moves to a "there" and "then" at Brideshead. Yet in this chapter Charles's awful London is a world that he, not his father, has created. At Brideshead he is greeted not by Sebastian but by Rex Mottram and a very different menagerie from the "ravening beasts" (79) that Sebastian had fantasized.

Waugh employs Charles's telephone conversation and train journey with Julia to frame the London sequence not only to reinforce the contrast between her and Celia but also to emphasize that Charles leaves not (as he had done in book 1, chapter 3) in flight but in a kind of triumph. His memories of the previous exhibition are used to establish a different kind of "then" and to serve as contrast to the present. Thus, while his new paintings may not be aesthetically successful, they have transformed ignorant condemnation to ignorant praise. And while his discovery of Celia's infidelity has given him emotional as well as physical freedom to separate himself from her, he has only a physical destination. Now he is going with Julia to Brideshead. In purely vindictive, worldly terms, he has reasserted his artistic and physical virility by convincing his critics and by openly leaving Celia.

Nevertheless, Charles's triumph is only partial because of the terms in which it is defined and the context in which it occurs. What he calls "Celia's Art and Fashion" (276) are also, however he may resist them, his own as well. The London sequence reinforces the connection between her energetic crassness and Charles's painting. Celia may be tasteless, but she is by no means stupid—she evaluates Samgrass quickly and accurately—and she pushes Charles's work tirelessly and efficiently without offending anyone but Charles. A less obvious point, though Ryder is careful to make it, is that the paintings are quite suited to Celia's promotional instincts and in fact meet the popular ideas of "Great Art." Thus, while Charles may be a bad painter, he is by no means a poor painter: his exhibition is clearly a social, financial, and critical success. Members of the Royal family attend; representatives of the wealthiest and most prestigious museums and foundations are going to buy his work; professional critics and popular audiences praise him with fulsome inaccuracy.

Anthony Blanche is reintroduced in this chapter because, although he may be partial, he is not inaccurate. He comes to bury Charles's reputation, not to praise it. Charles agrees with Blanche not only because Ryder has already, in the previous chapter, expressed in less memorable terms judgments at least as harsh, but also because the criticism serves as a kind of penance and, by destroying the old, leaves Charles free to move in new directions. But Charles's acquiescence to Anthony's judgments specifically does not include the indictment of charm (273), and though Charles does not overtly reject Anthony's strongly implied distinction between artistic and romantic success (269–70), the view of inspiration presented in the previous chapter is far removed from Anthony's.

Furthermore, Blanche's appearance establishes other perspectives of time and value. Charles need not overtly reject the indictment of charm because the values implied in contrast have brought Anthony to the Blue Grotto, which is condemned more in aesthetic than in moral terms. The temporal perspective evokes the visual memory of "Christ

Church meadow through a window of Ruskin Gothic" (271) and, like the memory of the stars sweeping "above the towers and gables of Oxford" (261) after the consummation of Charles and Julia's love, this memory allows Charles to establish a connection with his youth that is rare in book 2 but very important for the novel as a whole.

Still, although Charles can turn to Julia, he cannot at this point make a connection to "the old days" (274), which Rex invokes and which Brideshead, infected by "Rex's Politics and Money" (276) as Charles's painting is infected by Celia, cannot restore to him. In book 1, Charles was delivered from his father's persecution to the Arcadian refuge of Brideshead's spacious grounds and "a sense of liberation and peace" (78). Now, though Charles has freed himself from the oppressive world he helped to create, he and Julia are driven into a corner by the antiphonal lines of political bluster (in a technique probably borrowed from T. S. Eliot) about the Italian-Abyssinian War and the preabdication rumors about King Edward and Mrs. Simpson. And their "now" is as constricted as their "here" as they feel themselves at war with God and man and cling to "our happiness in spite of them; here and now" (276) with a bravado that they cannot really sustain.

CHAPTER 3

The most obvious structural feature of *Brideshead Revisited* is the disproportion in the lengths of books 1 and 2. Hostile critics, who tend to like the novel's early chapters, may react almost as much to the compression as to the content of book 2. It would not be fruitful to argue about content, but a closer examination of the method indicates that Waugh had a clear idea of what he was doing. Chapter 3 of book 2 is crucial to this argument because it shows the reasons for and ways in which Waugh is able to compress. The chapter repeats structural and thematic elements from book 1, especially from chapter 4, but the repetition is disguised by variations in tone. These variations are the result of the pressures of past and future (the two directions of "then") and the expanded and more threatening outside world ("there") both rendering more precarious the characters' sense of the here and now. Because of these pressures, the leisurely development and idyllic tone of book 1 is no longer possible.

The opening sequence by the fountain seems intended as a parallel to the langorous days at Brideshead with Sebastian in book 1, for in both chapters the "here" and "now" seem to enclose and dominate the "there" and "then" as they do in book 1, chapter 4. The world is defined in terms of the love affair and the time by counting the days that they have enjoyed in spite of the conspiracy they perceived at the end of chapter 2. Of course, the time is defined by negation: Julia and Charles count the days they have spent apart in the other, outer world instead of numbering the more than seven hundred days they have spent together. As in his first extended visit to Brideshead, Charles is content with the present, finding peace in the visual prospect before him. His attitude toward the fountain has changed: earlier, it was an object to study and admire (81, 82, 84) and occupied the foreground of the scene; here it serves as a backdrop for Julia (277), who is at the center of the carefully composed verbal portrait (279) lit by the dying sun as she is the center of Charles's painting. Charles has mastered the art to which in book 1 he was an apprentice, and he has learned to paint a human figure—which, as Bridey later says, without any sense of the deeper emotional engagement, is much more difficult than architectural painting—but he has not learned to see outside his frame or even to interpret all of the elements within it. Here, despite the end of the day and thus the passage of time, he perceives only the static moment and resists thoughts of "Plans, divorce, war—on an evening like this" (279).

In this chapter, Julia has replaced Sebastian, and like Sebastian she knows that the pastoral calm of Brideshead is threatened by "ravening beasts" and that the future holds more threat than promise. Julia sees farther and more clearly than her brother had done fourteen years earlier, partly because external circumstances are more obviously and publicly threatening. To Charles's praise of the illusory natural peace of the moment she responds first with the desire for "real peace" and then with the view of "the past and the future pressing so hard on either side that there's no room for the present at all" (279).

Lord Brideshead creates further pressure from both directions: his plans to live at Brideshead will dispossess Julia and Charles, and his matter-of-fact phrase about "living in sin" burdens Julia with the weight of her religious past. His function is obvious; the more interesting question is why Waugh took more space to re-introduce him than was devoted to his first appearance (88). There are at least two answers, structural and thematic. Waugh needed a kind of punctuation to separate the major dramatic scenes in the chapter, and he also needed to establish Bridey as a figure "without action" (280) and with "no spark of contemporary life in him" (282) to serve as a contrast with the thorough and despicable contemporaneity of Rex.

The extremes, defined in this way, would leave Julia and Charles comfortably at the mean. But through his engagement, Bridey enters time, and though in visual and social terms he may look ridiculous as a lover, his action gives a new perspective to Charles and Julia's affair because, in social and religious terms, they "*are* peculiar" (285). His doctrinally accurate label, "living in sin," forces Julia to see her own affair by absolute standards and, more important, to place it in the context not of the private, romantic world and the two previous years, which to Charles "seemed a lifetime" (286), but in the context of her whole life.

The phrase "in black and white," always associated with Bridey, is repeated three times (283, 286, 287) in the chapter. In the obvious sense, it refers to his habit of making sharp discriminations and unqualified judgments—there is no room for gray in his moral universe. But the phrase also refers literally to print—newspaper announcements of his engagement and religious tracts, both containing bare, factual discourse. This kind of language and the morality expressed in it may be accurate, but they are also inhuman.

Julia's speech about sin puts the moral issues in complex human terms. Waugh came to have doubts about this passage and about Lord Marchmain's final soliloquy. In comparing the two speeches he said in the preface to the 1960 edition that neither was "intended to repeat words actually spoken. They belong to a different way of writing from, say, the early scenes between Charles and his father. I would not now introduce them into a novel which elsewhere aims at verisimilitude. But I have retained them here . . . because . . . they were essentially of the mood of writing; also because many readers liked them, though that is not a consideration of first importance" (9–10).

Like other critics of the novel, Waugh may have been unduly harsh because he does not deal with the construction of Julia's soliloquy or with the way in which it functions in the novel as a whole. First, the passage has two distinct parts, divided by the paragraph at the middle of page 287. In the first half, Julia speaks for herself, composing a setting for the pamphlet, defining the term "living in sin" as opposed to committing sin, and personifying sin first as a kind of double of herself and then as an "idiot child." The first embodiment echoes the idea, already applied to Rex and to Charles, that to live outside the spiritual world is to be only partly human. The second recalls Julia's guilty feeling that her stillborn child is a judgment on her marriage to Rex (259) and anticipates her desire to have a child in order to complete some kind of pattern (291).

The second half of Julia's soliloquy, more lyric in tone, associational in development, and surrealistic in imagery, is in fact not her speech but Ryder's construction from "single words and broken sentences" (287). As the subsequent interlude will show, Charles as actor is incapable of providing a system of values or a syntax to give shape to these fragments; twice he is described as without guidance or direction, as if at sea (288, 290). Bridey's "black-and-white" words provide a doctrinal outline; Julia's images move from personal to traditional images of the burden of sin. "Now"—the two years of her love for Charles—can no longer be separated from "then," for time is seen under the aspect, and judgment, of eternity. The "there" of the castle becomes not Brideshead but Eden, heaven, the hall of the king's wedding feast (Matt. 22: 11–14) from which Julia is exiled to "here," a wasteland garbage dump in exterior darkness in which the central object is the dead child with which she is obsessed. This passage and the vision it embodies belong neither to Bridey nor to Julia: only Ryder as narrator is able to connect past with present, personal experience with religious value, form with content, idea and vocabulary with syntax, word with flesh.

Indirectly, the passage serves to remind the reader that Charles is not yet Ryder. The distinction is emphasized by Charles's admission that he "was as far from her in spirit . . . as when years ago I had lit her cigarette on the way from the station [76]; as far as when she was out of mind, in the dry, empty years at the Old Rectory and in the jungle" (288)—in other words, when he was part of a man pretending to be a whole. He cannot remember any security or wholeness outside Julia's love. Therefore, he resorts to seeing things secondhand, in purely aesthetic terms. He alludes to Ruskin's description of Holman Hunt's "The Awakened Conscience" as an example of Victorian camp without spiritual dimension. He sees the events of the evening as a play whose scenes are set at the fountain, unable to see the importance or even the relevance of the religious themes introduced in the intervals.

In contrast, Julia has at least begun to move toward an integration of past and present. Like Sebastian two hundred pages earlier, she wishes that religion was "all bosh" (290), but her desire for "some sort of order in a human way" (291) and her desire to marry Charles retreat from the vision expressed in her soliloquy. However, that vision has qualified her earlier desire for "real peace" (279) because, as her reference to "the Last Trump" indicates, she has begun to recognize that human order will be ended not merely by war but by God's judgment.

That recognition is only partial at this point, and she is not prepared to act on it, but Charles's failure to comprehend her motivates her angry rejection of his aesthetic and detached viewpoint and her blows to his face. Out of love, stoicism, helpless incomprehension, or all three, Charles literally obeys the biblical injunction (Matt. 5:39; Luke 6:28) to turn the other cheek and sees her to bed. The movement of her lips against the pillow, whether a goodnight or a prayer transmitted through Nanny Hawkins from centuries of tradition (292–93), contrasts markedly with the image near the end of chapter 2 of Julia's "little sigh of ease—a sigh fit for the pillow, the sinking firelight and a bedroom window open to the stars and the whisper of bare trees" (274). Now time has passed and full summer has not brought fulfillment; now the context is not romantic but spiritual; now Julia is seen not as a lover but as a child. And though neither Charles nor Ryder says so, Charles acts from kindness and even, in the theological sense, charity.

The immediate incursion of Rex and his colleagues recalls the passage near the end of the previous chapter, but here the issues are more serious than King Edward's desire to marry Mrs. Simpson, and the talk is more bellicose. The final scenes of these two chapters, with Julia and Charles set apart from the antiphonal, self-serving rhetoric, are also similar. At the end of chapter 2, however, the couple could speculate on how many nights lay before them. Here, supported by the allusion to the failed romance of Troilus and Cressida, time is compressed into "A lifetime between the rising of the moon and its setting. Then the dark" (295).

CHAPTER 4

This chapter begins the process, completed in chapter 5, of turning the novel's focus from romance to theology and preparing Charles, and the reader, for the possibility that his love for Julia may neither triumph nor endure. The movement away from the personal is reflected in the chapter's construction: interludes between Charles and Julia punctuate scenes that give Charles new and disquieting perspectives on his love for Julia.

Part of the difference in tone and narrative movement between chapters 3 and 4 may be explained by the somewhat cynical view that although adultery may be romantic, divorce is not. At the beginning of chapter 4, as in chapter 3, Waugh has to deal with the problem of regaining narrative movement because he has succeeded in creating a dying fall at the end of the previous chapter. In chapter 3, he solved the problem by having Julia and Charles look back nostalgically, counting the days that they have wrested from the conspiracy against them, a period which, the rest of the chapter demonstrates, is the best part of their romantic idyll. Chapter 3 begins with a rhetorical question, in an idyllic scene, answered by an antiphonal list of memories. In contrast, chapter 4 begins with a series of bald, practical statements about the divorce settlement by Boy Mulcaster that are punctuated by Charles's one-line responses.

This is the first of four brief scenes, presented in a technique like the cinematic montages Waugh had used in earlier novels like *A Handful of Dust,* that establish the social view of Charles's and Julia's divorces. All of the dialogue emphasizes dissolution and dispersal rather than the "human order" that Julia envisioned; and the first three people to speak to Charles use "happily" and "happy" with an unconscious irony and establish a counterpoint to that desire. Mulcaster blandly stage-manages his sister's divorce from Charles; Edward Ryder and Rex Mottram resist, for different reasons, the disturbance of the status quo; and Beryl, as good Catholic bride-to-be, gives qualified approval to the new pairings.

Then, as Waugh had often done in earlier novels, he puts the scenes in a larger context: here "private affairs" are placed within the context of the "general alarm" (298) of the political crisis of 1938. This crisis led to the temporary, essentially unprincipled, and thoroughly unstable agreement between Neville Chamberlain and Hitler, which resulted in the dismemberment of Czechoslovakia in an attempt to avoid a general European war. Waugh may be subtly comparing Chamberlain's futile maneuverings with the negotiations and logistical moves of the two divorces on the personal level.

He certainly establishes—resurrecting Cousin Jasper for the purpose—Julia and Charles as "an old story." The first interlude between the pair indicates small joy in their future as they view the magnificent terrace of Brideshead, now choked with dead leaves, and contemplate returning, "Perhaps years later, to what's left of it, with what's left of us" (299–300). The conclusions of chapters 2 and 3 presented external and immediate threats. Here Julia recognizes the possibility that the threat may be internal and their fate less dramatic. The energy—never very great on Julia's part—that has carried them through the affair and into the process of divorce is at this point expended.

Cordelia's return creates a new source of narrative energy and a series of new contexts. At first, Charles judges her by his familiar romantic and aesthetic standards. He regrets "all that burning love spending itself on serum injections and delousing powder." He thinks her "an ugly woman" (300) in appearance and movement, judging Cordelia by the standards of "Julia's white skin and silk and jewelled hair" (301) and romantic fulfillment. He also contrasts her present appearance with his memories of her in a further attempt to separate past from present.

The rest of the chapter alters Charles's explicit views of Cordelia and his implicit views of the past. First, the characters make the obligatory visit to Nanny Hawkins, but Waugh has created a subtle change in the reader's attitude towards her. In earlier scenes, Nanny has obvious associations with the Flytes' childhoods, giving an uncritical love that is necessary but unavailing against the world outside the nursery. At the beginning of book 1, Sebastian finds in her and in the nursery a kind of order and comfort nowhere else available to him, especially not from his mother. At the appalling Christmas party that precedes Sebastian's exile, Nanny's limitations as well as her value are emphasized: visited by her charges (though never Brideshead, who is bound in duty beyond the claims of mere human affection), she likes to "watch their faces and think of them as she had known them as small children; their present goings-on did not signify much beside those early illnesses and crimes" (151). For Julia (see pages 259, 287, 293), Nanny is specifically associated with the traditional religion learned in childhood, but unlike her brother, she sees their mother as continuing Nancy's teaching and example in a more complex way (288).

In this scene, Waugh has Ryder insist upon the comparison of Nanny with Ryder's father as "two people who seemed impervious to change" (301). The comparison qualifies her symbolic value, for it indicates that change may not be entirely bad and that the inability to change, or to understand and accept change, is a limitation unsuited to adulthood whether it is caused by uncritical female warmth or selfish male indifference.

Yet the scene with Nanny does give Charles a new perspective on Cordelia. Though he does not find her any more beautiful in conventional physical terms than before, he does see "her fond eyes on all of us" and realizes that she has "a beauty of her own" (302). This contrast is often used as a cliché—"She's a beautiful *person*" has a code value in everyday language, but Waugh uses it here to indicate that Charles has begun to value not what he sees but the way in which another person sees—which for him is a major shift in attitude.

Cordelia gives a capsule account of Sebastian, tailored to Nanny's scale of nursery values, but the other characters have more complex responses to what Sebastian was and is. The interlude between the lovers deals explicitly with Sebastian's place in Charles's emotional development, and for the first time, in the extended image of pursuing a shadow (303), Charles considers that love of Julia may not be an end in itself. This passage represents a significant change in the figurative language of the novel. At the beginning of book 2, shadows—"abstractions and reflections and counterfeits of ourselves"—were to be escaped by fleeing into a private, asocial world where the essential self could exist unencumbered (225–26). Here the shadow is something to pursue out of a sense that the self can be completed not by separation and isolation but by movement toward union. Union with what or whom is not, at this point, made clear, but the idea has been firmly established. The idea that Sebastian is the forerunner is used not merely to connect this scene with chapter 1 of book 2, but also to color, in ways that will not be fully apparent until the end of chapter 5, Cordelia's account of Sebastian's present way of life.

Cordelia's narrative of that life, which develops further the theme of flight and pursuit, is accomplished with great technical dexterity. Various accounts—official, from the consul; personal, from the Greeks; spiritual, from the Superior—prepare for the entrance of Sebastian and his selfless account of Kurt. And Cordelia's voice is subtly varied to suit character and tone. In broader terms, Sebastian's admission that he needs a missionary for himself recalls, but is a major progression from, the image of Sebastian as innocent pagan whose world—of which the teddy bear is emblem—was destroyed by the incursion of missionaries.

Charles remembers "the joyful youth with the Teddy-bear under the flowering chestnuts" (309) and laments his degeneration, but Cordelia implies an opposition between Arcadian aestheticism and the concept of suffering; to charm, grace; and to happiness, holiness. The world in which she lives—not just the historical world of the Spanish Civil War and the approaching world war but the fallen human world redeemed by God's grace—is a sterner and more coherent world than the private Arcadia envisioned by Charles, whether he shared it with Sebastian or with Julia. (The mocking ghost of Anthony Blanche is raised and dismissed by placing his account of Cordelia's governess's suicide in this new context [308].) Although she makes a concession to Charles's aesthetic viewpoint by describing the beautiful setting of the monastery, she insists that Sebastian does suffer and that the suffering has a value greater than earthly beauty or happiness.

Even more explicitly, she reverses Charles's judgment of her as "thwarted" and applies the term to him and Julia. Her viewpoint gives Charles a new perspective on Julia in the chapter's final interlude involving the lovers. Although as an object she is as beautiful to con-template as ever, Charles realizes that she has "regained . . . the magi-cal sadness which had drawn me to her, the thwarted look that had seemed to say, 'Surely I was made for some other purpose than this?' " (310). "Regained," usually applied to the recovery of something valu-able, seems an odd word in this context, but Waugh uses it to indicate that the sadness, like Sebastian's suffering, may have value on a scale that Charles cannot yet read. More immediately important, he has learned to see Julia, as he has Cordelia, not as an object but as a person, not as something static but as someone moving toward or rather in need of a goal. Though distanced from her as a lover, he sees her more clearly.

As the last section of the chapter indicates, Charles sees her more clearly than he does himself. As he does whenever he wishes to portray a complex and partially understood mental state, he turns to extended figures of speech. The image of the horse refusing a jump indicates not just his inability but his unwillingness to understand the obstacle to his desires. The next, and more fully developed, image implies that mere understanding is not going to help Charles. The impending avalanche that threatens the little private world—here the world of solitary com-fort rather than shared love—is impersonal and inexorable. The previous two chapters concluded with threats to shared happiness; here Charles is left with nothing to cling to.

CHAPTER 5

In almost leisurely fashion, chapter 5 not only accomplishes the destruction of Charles's hopes for romantic love in elegant surroundings isolated from the confusions and conflicts and the aesthetic disharmonies of the external world, but it also indicates the final stages of the process by which Charles becomes Ryder, the past becomes the present, the little world of Brideshead is subsumed into the world of war—and, in the shorthand of the subtitles used in some English editions, "the purpose revealed" changes from romantic to eschatological. Not surprisingly, this chapter is more complexly ordered than any of its predecessors. Earlier chapters could be reduced to a single linear structure because Charles thought in that way. In this chapter Charles is very reluctantly turned from spectator to participant. He does not perceive the process. Ryder does, but Waugh subordinates his narrator's superior knowledge in order to prepare for the fusion of actor and narrator into Charles Ryder.

Also, of course, chapter 5 presents the climax and a kind of conclusion. In a sense, the conclusion of any narrative uses up by exhausting or bringing to fulfillment the time and the space of the narrative. To put it more simply, the book ends because nothing more can or need be said. Older novels, like Henry Fielding's *Tom Jones* or William Makepeace Thackeray's *Vanity Fair,* end with a summary in which the characters are fixed, set in a frame apart from personal or social history. Evelyn Waugh respected the craftsmanship of traditional novelists, but because his respect went beyond imitation, he adapted their methods to create his own vision. In a fashion more subtle than modernist forbears like T. S. Eliot and James Joyce, he puts the devices of art at the more or less conscious (or self-conscious) control of a character within the work.

In chapter 5, Lord Marchmain functions as the artist struggling to control his material, to order what he can in a world closing in upon him, and, by arranging objects and people in space, to halt the process of his own decline. In the elaborate and complicated second sentence of the chapter, which takes nine lines to get to the key verb and object, "declared his intention," Lord Marchmain seizes control of the action, buries Charles even more deeply in the role of spectator, and (brilliantly realized by Lord Olivier in the television version of *Brideshead Revisited*) takes center stage so firmly that the other actors are pushed nearly to the wings.

In the early stages of the chapter (which are signalled by blank spaces in the text), Lord Marchmain is not merely the star actor but, at times, the director and even the set designer. His mere decision to return to Brideshead changes the pageant scenario from "the marriage of the heir" to "the return of the lord of the manor." The first three pages of the chapter present the logistical consequences of his decision. They also delay, for purposes of dramatic emphasis, the entrance of the star to a carefully prepared set and atmosphere—and Waugh milks his entrance (describing first his figure, then his features, then his movements, then his costume change, and then, anticlimactically, his speech [314–15]) to emphasize first his loss of control and then his reassertion of it.

Like a shrewd actor, Lord Marchmain makes a virtue of his own limitations. Unable to move further, he creates a stage set of the hall, actually sitting on "a little heraldic chair" which is not just "a mere excuse for the elaborate armorial painting on its back" (315) but is in fact a sign of his power as well as a physical center from which the others must radiate. From this vantage, he can "give orders" for the carefully designed set of his bedroom and thus, himself motionless, create motion from which, vicariously, he can draw life. His exit line for the first section—" 'You might paint it, eh—and call it "The Death Bed"?' "—is a brilliantly managed dramatic stroke. As the content of the speech indicates, however, he is less interested in completing the plot than in framing a still life in all the complicated senses of that term, which may include aesthetic order and vital signs.

Of course, Lord Marchmain knows at one level that he must die, and he seeks to establish by his will (a pun that Waugh at least intends) a future for his Brideshead in which Julia rather than Lord Brideshead will be the focus. By "installing Julia . . . so beautiful always; much, much more suitable" (321) rather than her righteous brother and his unappealing wife, he will enforce aesthetic rather than moral principles. Thus he intends to re-create Brideshead in his own image, as he fancies it existed before Lady Marchmain and her Catholic faith brought the knowledge of good and evil that drove him from the paradise of his ancestral home. In this view, the chapel becomes "the last of the new house to come, the first to go" (334).

This passage comes near the end of Lord Marchmain's long monologue, the last words he speaks. In the preface to the 1960 edition, Waugh indicated that, like Julia's speech about "living in sin" in chapter 3, this was not "intended to report words actually spoken" but that both "were essentially of the mood of writing" (9–10). Both speeches also had important functions in the novel's understructure. The first presents a vision of an unredeemable wasteland in the future; the second embodies a vision of an aristocratic past while in effect enclosing and ending time and history and reducing the broad and opulent space of the estate to a cave or dungeon inhabited by static and aestheticized figures of men who do not need to breathe and whose presence makes Lord Marchmain realize that he cannot live in the artfully ordered world that, as shown by the image of the dry fountain and the reed-choked lakes, he imagines his death will end.

Charles had, or wished to have, an imaginative kinship with Lord Marchmain from their first meeting in Venice (book 1, chapter 4), and it might be argued that Charles as an adult models his conversational style on the older man's because he recognizes the "frame of malevolence under his urbanity," shares the first, and wishes to assume the second. In this chapter, he identifies with Lord Marchmain because he thinks, and hopes, that their interests are identical and because they both cling to a conception of the will as capable of ordering and controlling.

In fact, Charles in his architectural painting and Lord Marchmain in his soliloquy function in much the same way: both draw upon and memorialize a past that can be preserved only in aesthetic terms. When Lord Marchmain has created the stage set, the Queen's bed in the Chinese room, for his lying-in-state, he turns to Charles for approval because he knows that Charles will appreciate his imaginative ordering of the materials and sympathize with his desire to subsume his death into a kind of art. Julia's view that Charles must "see everything secondhand" (291), by analogy to forms of art, also applies to her father.

The tendency of both men to distance themselves from experience by allusive analogy is underlined in a passage early in the chapter. Watching Lord Marchmain in his bed, Charles notes the "Hogarthian aspect" of the room (318). William Hogarth, the eighteenth-century English artist best known today for "The Rake's Progress," was a fierce moralist who set against material opulence the physical decay and by extension the moral degeneracy of the people he portrayed. As if subliminally aware of these disquieting overtones, Charles turns to the physical decor and draws from the amoral and magical Christmas pantomime for children the analogy with the scenery "of Aladdin's cave" (319).

Lord Marchmain then draws upon a more exalted source in asking Cordelia to "watch for an hour in this Gethsemane" (319). On the surface, Lord Marchmain is dramatizing his state of mind as he approaches death, but Waugh expects his readers to be aware of the allusion's full weight. The night before the Crucifixion, Christ went into the garden of Gethsemane to pray, first that his agony of spirit would be lifted and finally, with "not my will, but thine, be done" (Luke 22:42), to submit His will to that of His Father. This conception of the will is very different from that which orders people and things in life or art and from the "wonderful will to live" that Charles praises in Lord Marchmain and the doctor redefines as "a great fear of death" that exhausts the dying man (331).

Charles is not at this point able to understand the distinction, perhaps because he is blinded by a will in another sense. When Lord Marchmain decides to leave Brideshead Castle not to his elder son but to Julia, Charles sees the inheritance as opening a prospect; the prospect one gained at the turn of the avenue, as I had first seen it with Sebastian, of the secluded valley, the lakes falling away one below the other, the old house in the foreground, the rest of the world abandoned and forgotten; a world of its own of peace and love and beauty; a soldier's dream in a foreign bivouac; such a prospect perhaps as a high pinnacle of the temple afforded after the hungry days in the desert and the jackal-haunted nights. Need I reproach myself if sometimes I was rapt in the vision? (321–22)

The desire for "peace and love and beauty" is not reprehensible; it is merely impossible. First, the various allusions to the coming war—which, Ryder and the reader know, will begin in September, when Julia's divorce is final—show that the "order in human way" (291) that Julia desired will be impossible. Second, Lord Marchmain's decline shows the instability of all merely human structures. Julia at times "seemed to throw herself against the restraints of her love for me like a caged animal against the bars" (330), and Lord Marchmain imagines Brideshead reduced to an airless dungeon, like "Aladdin's treasury" (333). For them, a refuge has become a trap.

Although the parts blend too well to allow for a sharp division, it can be argued that the first part of the chapter is devoted to describing the trap, the second to finding a way out. Looked at in this way, the chapter is not about Lord Marchmain, who cannot imagine a way out, or Charles, who refuses to consider a way out, but about Julia, who resists taking the way that she has always known.

On the surface, the conflict, as in all drama, concerns what to *do*. In this case, Lord Marchmain does not want to see a priest and receive absolution for his sins. Charles supports this decision, ostensibly out of loyalty to the old man's wishes. Cordelia and Lord Brideshead take the orthodox view. For much of the chapter, Julia is a silent or reluctant witness.

In narrative or dramatic structure, as in fairy tales about the third and youngest brother, the most important events happen three times. Here the priest appears three times, but not quite in straightforward chronological fashion. The issue is, characteristically, raised by Lord

Brideshead "in his heavy, ruthless way": "Papa must see a priest" (324). As the page-long flashback reveals, the unnamed parish priest has already paid a visit and been politely turned away because, Cordelia says, "Papa doesn't want him yet." The "yet" troubles Charles, but he can get neither support nor disagreement from Julia, and the religious issue is imaged as a cloud presaging a storm.

Bridey never has doubts about anything, and here as always he is useful for moving the action forward; and as usual he fails to accomplish his end. Waugh does not present the priest's visit directly: Charles learns of Lord Marchmain's repudiation of spiritual comfort in fragments of conversation heard, significantly, through a closed door and receives Cordelia's report as, rooted as firmly in the material world as she is in the spiritual, she eats a strip of bacon. Charles perceives the outcome not in terms of the principle but in terms of the person stating it. Earlier he has said to Bridey, "if I ever felt for a moment like becoming a Catholic, I should only have to talk to you for five minutes to be cured" (164). Here Charles reduces the theological issues to a contest between Bridey and himself, and he reports Bridey's failure to Julia in schoolboy slang with almost obscene triumph at the discomfiture of the pious. He also is able to confess, as Ryder judging Charles, his elation at "another unexpressed, inexpressible, indecent little victory that I was furtively celebrating" (328)—because he and Bridey are also rivals for Lord Marchmain's material estate.

Bridey is unconscious of, and would probably be unconcerned about, his father's disposition of his estate in a last will and testament, but his will in another sense is very important to all of the characters. Waugh uses Charles to summarize the doctrine of the last sacraments not only to avoid the legalistic exposition that Bridey presumably gives but also to indicate that Charles fully understands and gives a quite orthodox account of the importance of Lord Marchmain's "act of will" (329) in being reconciled with God.

But at this point, Charles's understanding is abstract, and as in earlier scenes, he attempts to place Julia on his side, against "these people" (330). Julia resists this attempt and struggles, as she had done in chapter 3, against the constraints of her love for Charles. The final visit of the priest reveals that the theological conflict must be worked out between the lovers in personal terms.

The image of Julia as "a caged animal" is echoed on the following page by Charles's comment on the pretense that the anticipated "emergency" has no connection with "an act of human will; nothing so clear and simple as wrath or retribution; an emergency; something coming out of the waters, a monster with sightless face and thrashing tail thrown up from the depths" (331). But the war, like Julia's "brief accesses of hate" (330), is connected with human inability to will the highest good. Here and in the following passage, which contrasts the coming world war with Lord Marchmain's "solitary struggle to keep alive," Waugh implies the connection between private sin and public evil.

The apparently casual comings and goings of Bridey and Cordelia create the circumstances in which Julia alone is forced to choose between Charles and her faith. This time, though Charles is not consulted, he is not an unseen auditor on the other side of a closed door. Instead he is a witness to and finally a participant in an action that is stripped, by omission and implication, of its scenery and, as the disappearance of proper nouns for two paragraphs indicates, is beyond mere personality in "the universal drama in which there is only one actor" (338). And for the first time in the novel, both Charles and Ryder focus intensely on the here and now without yearning for another time or place.

Perhaps for the first time, Charles is participating in his own drama—moving from the double conditionals of his first, agnostic prayer to the desire for an answer to another's prayer to a direct and unconditional petition from his own need. When Lord Marchmain—the proper name is used, perhaps, to indicate that the individual, not the generic man, is saved—makes the sign of the cross, Charles Ryder acknowledges and accepts a new kind of inheritance that is spiritual rather than legal. In the allusion to "the veil of the temple being rent from top to bottom" (Matt. 27:51; Mark 15:38, King James version) at the moment of Christ's death on the cross, Ryder accepts a new vision and a whole new world.

The completeness of his acceptance is made clear in the final scene with Julia. When she attempts to explain in theological terms, though not to justify, her decision to live apart from Charles, he has already understood: "Since this morning; since before this morning; all this year" (340). In this as in the rest of the novel, outward action changes nothing, and as Waugh indicates by the title of book 2, "A Twitch upon the Thread," the characters are drawn to an end that was always there, could not be avoided, and must be recognized and accepted.

This is simpler to state in dramatic than in psychological terms. Julia and Charles know what they will not do, but they have no notion of what they will do in living out the consequences of their decision. The final paragraph completes the image of the avalanche introduced at the end of chapter 4: "The avalanche was down, the hillside swept bare behind it; the last echoes died on the white slopes; the new mound glittered and lay still in the silent valley" (341). Nothing remains of the "little lighted place" that was "dry and neat and warm inside" (310, 311). But Charles Ryder is alive to complete the image, and the brightness and silence of the new world imply at least the possibility of hope.

11

Finding a Future

On 6 June 1944, D-day for the Allied forces invading Normandy, Evelyn Waugh noted in his diary that he had "sat down early to work and wrote a fine passage of Lord Marchmain's death agonies," was interrupted by his landlady bearing news of the invasion, and "worked through till 4 o'clock and finished the last chapter. . . . There only remains now the epilogue which is easy meat" (*Diaries*, 567–68). Given the many structural and thematic elements that the epilogue had to resolve, Waugh's confidence must have come not from the simplicity of the task but from his sense that he was in full control of his material.

Of course, in writing the prologue, Waugh had already defined the major terms and movements of the epilogue. The prologue had moved from bleak present to aesthetically harmonious past, from the "planless maze" (7) of the Pollock camp to the slope of the Bride valley, "still unravished" (16), which Ryder faces as he leaves his hut to stand "between two realities and two dreams," wondering "Which was the mirage, which the palpable earth?" (16). "Still unravished" is a direct and inescapably obvious quotation from the opening line of John Keats's "Ode on a Grecian Urn." The urn, addressed in the opening line as

"Thou still unravished bride of quietness," contains a static picture of a youth pursuing a girl whom he will never possess but also never lose. At the end of the poem, the poet sees the urn as emblematizing romantic longing and aesthetic completeness fused into an unchanging harmony that says to the contemplator (or—punctuation and interpretations differ—merely to the urn, or the equations to the contemplator and the rest to the urn): "Beauty is truth, truth beauty", that is all / Ye know on earth, and all ye need to know."

But the closing lines of the prologue and the rest of the novel indicate quite clearly that this is not all that Charles Ryder needs to know. The beauty of the landscape and the truth of his spiritual desolation cannot at this point be fused into a whole.

The last lines of the prologue indicate a method rather than arrive at a solution. Hooper, Ryder's incredibly incompetent subaltern, tells him about a chapel, "More in your line than mine," and

> "a frightful great fountain too, in front of the steps, all rocks and sort of carved animals. You never saw such a thing."
> "Yes, Hooper, I did. I've been here before."
> The words seemed to ring back to me enriched from the vaults of my dungeon.
> "Oh well, you know all about it. I'll go and get cleaned up."
> I had been there before; I knew all about it. (17)

The closing sentence juxtaposes Ryder's words with Hooper's. The tonal shading is crucial to the novel, and although Ryder is quite capable of sarcasm, the tone is not quite sarcastic. The hopelessly unromantic Hooper prompts Ryder to the first open statement about his past experience (which, in the epilogue, he will not acknowledge to his commanding officer). But Hooper cannot know what Ryder knows about it, and in fact, as most of the prologue indicates quite clearly, what Ryder knows has failed to sustain him because he has not, in the full sense, recalled it.

The body of the novel presents that recollection, and the passage about memory at the beginning of book 2 indicates that the content of memory is less important than the process of remembering. Ryder goes beyond his personal experience to assert the general principle that "These memories are the memorials and pledges of the vital hours of a lifetime," which are "the springs of art" (225). Only by experiencing these moments, and by ordering them in art or contemplation, is the human being fully alive.

Up to the end of the prologue, Ryder has been unable to recall and re-create and therefore he has been unable to free himself from the dungeon of his present. An understanding of this state, and of the process that he undertakes, helps to answer a question that has vexed a number of critics: If Ryder has already become a Roman Catholic before his narration begins, then why does he have to revisit Brideshead to be reminded that the desolation of his present world is trivial when seen under the aspect of eternity? One answer seems obvious: only people without experience of the spiritual life imagine that it is ceaselessly and unchangingly consoling. Religious people live in the world, and sometimes that world is almost unbearably depressing. At the beginning of the prologue, Ryder sees himself not as a believer but as a soldier, and that role has failed him.

To be able to imagine himself as whole, he returns to his past in the body of the novel. The epilogue is more than the completion of a circular structure because it allows Ryder to see the present not just through the perspective of nostalgia or even of precise memory but of hope in the future which acknowledges both present and past and makes them parts of a larger pattern.

In order to create this process, Waugh uses structural patterns and verbal echoes from Ryder's past. Most significantly, the arrangement of incidents in the epilogue reflects but does not reproduce that of Charles's first visit to Brideshead and interweaves other allusions to establish a counterpoint between present and past. That first visit is marked by Sebastian's saying "not 'That is my home,' but 'It's where my family live' " (35), but the chill is dispelled by the visit to Nanny's nursery domain in the dome of the great house, her profile against the spacious harmony of the grounds. Charles is allowed the briefest glimpse of the public rooms, and his tour ends in the chapel (34–39).

The epilogue has a different kind of internal structure. It begins with the commanding officer's judgement that, because of the isolation of the estate, which Charles had valued at first sight and ever after, this is "The worst place we've struck yet." He then announces his plans to use as a mortar range the "still unravished" slope of the valley. The quartering commandant who gives Ryder the guided tour and inventory of the interior of Brideshead is much more sympathetic to its beauty than the commanding officer, or for that matter Sebastian. Yet he is unable to preserve the artifacts—most lamentably, from his point of view, Charles's paintings in the garden-room—from military vandalism.

The view of the badly damaged terrace and "the dry basin of the fountain" (347), which ends this tour, is obviously intended to recall the first presentation of the terrace as "the final consummation of the house's plan" (80) and of the fountain, which had caused Charles to feel "a whole new system of nerves alive within me, as though the water that spurted and bubbled among its stones was indeed a life-giving spring" (82). This passage used the image of baptism to describe aesthetic conversion; now the baptismal font is dry. From this point Ryder moves to Nanny Hawkins's stronghold. But she, like the fountain, has changed, and she cannot, as she had in the past, serve as emotional center or source of renewal.

The chapel is the final stop on the tours of Brideshead that are twenty years apart. In 1923, Charles can respond to this "monument of art nouveau" only with "Golly," and though he does copy Sebastian's sign of the cross, he does so out of politeness rather than conviction. Later, Cordelia applies the opening line of the biblical book of Lamentations, "*Quomodo sedet sola civitas*" ("How doth the city sit solitary that was full of people") to link with the destruction of Jerusalem and the temple her feeling about the deconsecration of the chapel and the loss of the family's spiritual center.

On this visit, however, the vital flame in the chapel's "beaten-copper lamp of deplorable design" (351) not only serves as a sign that the equally appalling tabernacle contains a consecrated Host (to Catholics the actual substance of the Body and Blood of Christ) but it also serves as a contrast to and consolation for the dry fountain. Having, by implication, undergone a conversion from the sensual world to the spiritual, Ryder no longer needs the fountain. While fully aware of the chapel's aesthetic shortcomings, instead of criticizing its surface, he says a prayer and meditates on the spiritual implications—not just for himself but for all humanity, Crusaders of romance and modern enlisted men—of the relit lamp and on the manner in which human intentions are transfigured by divine purpose.

Even before he visits the chapel, he is able to see his experience as part of a pattern. In the prologue he contemplated a landscape that "had been planned and planted a century and a half ago so that, at about this date, it might be seen in its maturity" (16). In the epilogue, he remembers Sebastian's "It is where my family live" and thinks his own comment that Brideshead "belongs to friends of mine" is odd because the sentence can embody only palely the depth of his involvement. But in telling Hooper "I'm homeless, childless, middle-aged, loveless" (350), he confesses his own failure to participate in basic human processes. Like the sharp contrast in Ryder's response to his subordinate's unmilitary "Rightyoh" (10, 350), this confession indicates a shift in Ryder's attitude which does him good, however little it affects Hooper.

On the last page of the epilogue, as in the prologue, Ryder is able to juxtapose elements of the past and the present. Earlier he could only place them side by side and look toward the past. Here he recalls "*Quomodo sedet sola civitas*" and, from Ecclesiastes, "Vanity of vanities, all is vanity." But he rejects both sentiments and for the first time responds to the military present of the bugle's plain and plebian mess call. As he moves back into military routine, he sees not two realities and two dreams but a vision of romantic past and bleak future, human purpose and divine plan, himself as soldier and spiritual being, as parts of a complex whole. No wonder he quickens his pace and looks "unusually cheerful" as the novel ends.

Notes and References

1. *Work Suspended* (London: Chapman and Hall, 1942), 11; hereafter cited in the text. The novel has been republished, with a few revisions and many deletions, several times. The most accessible is *Work Suspended and Other Stories including Charles Ryder's Schooldays* (Harmondsworth, England: Penguin, 1982).

2. *The Diaries of Evelyn Waugh*, ed. Michael Davie (Boston: Little, Brown, n.d.), 438; hereafter cited in the text.

3. *The End of the Battle* (Boston: Little, Brown, 1961), 245.

4. *The Essays, Articles and Reviews of Evelyn Waugh*, ed. Donat Gallagher (Boston: Little, Brown, 1984), 302–3; hereafter cited in the text.

5. Chaim Potok, "The Role of the Jewish Artist: As Jew, as Citizen, as Craftsman," *Congress Bi-Weekly* 74 (1974):307.

6. *The Letters of Evelyn Waugh*, ed. Mark Amory (New Haven, Conn., and New York: Ticknor & Fields, 1980), 180, 200; hereafter cited in the text.

7. "Warning," reprinted in Harold C. Gardiner, "Follow-up on Waugh," *America* 74 (1946):536.

8. For a selection of reviews of *Brideshead Revisited*, see *Evelyn Waugh: The Critical Heritage*, ed. Martin Stannard (London and Boston: Routledge & Kegan Paul, 1984), 233–87. Edmund Wilson's laudatory " 'Never Apologize, Never Explain': The Art of Evelyn Waugh' and his condemnation of *Brideshead Revisited*, "Splendors and Miseries of Evelyn Waugh" (*New Yorker*, 5 January 1946, 71–74), are reprinted in his collection *Classics and Commercials* (New York: Vintage, 1962).

9. Marston LaFrance, "Context and Structure of Evelyn Waugh's *Brideshead Revisited*," *Twentieth Century Literature* 10 (1964):18.

10. D. S. Savage, "The Innocence of Evelyn Waugh," *Western Review* 14 (1950):199, 203.

11. The reviews by Macaulay, O'Donnell (O'Brien), and Kermode are reprinted in *Evelyn Waugh: The Critical Heritage*. Sean O'Faolain, *The Vanish-*

ing Hero: Studies in Novelists of the Twenties (Boston: Little, Brown, 1957), 39.

12. Inna Levidova, "At an Englishman's Home," *Soviet Literature* no. 11 (1974):156–58.

13. Henry Reed, untitled review, *New Statesman and Nation*, 25 June 1945, 408–9 (reprinted in *Evelyn Waugh: The Critical Heritage*, 240): LaFrance, 16; David Lodge, *Evelyn Waugh* (New York and London: Columbia University Press, 1971), 33.

14. Joseph Hynes, "Varieties of Death Wish: Evelyn Waugh's Central Theme," *Criticism* 14 (1973):65–77; John Edward Hardy, "*Brideshead Revisited:* God, Man, and Others," *Man in the Modern Novel* (Seattle: University of Washington Press, 1964), 159–74; Thomas Prufer, "The Death of Charm and the Advent of Grace: Waugh's *Brideshead Revisited,*" *Communio* 10 (1983):281–91; Jeffrey Heath, *The Picturesque Prison: Evelyn Waugh and His Writing* (Kingston and Montreal: McGill-Queen's University Press, 1982), 161–62.

15. John Coleman, untitled review, *Spectator*, 29 July 1960, 187 (reprinted in *The Critical Heritage*, 276–78); Edward Pearce, "*Brideshead Revisited:* Chronicles of a Social Alpinist," *Encounter* 58 (March 1982):48–50; Jeffrey Heath, "*Brideshead:* The Critics and the Memorandum," *English Studies* 56 (1975):224–25.

16. James Carens, *The Satiric Art of Evelyn Waugh* (Seattle: University of Washington Press, 1966); Federick J. Stopp, *Evelyn Waugh: Portrait of an Artist* (Boston: Little, Brown, 1958); William J. Cook, Jr., *Masks, Modes, and Morals: The Art of Evelyn Waugh* (Rutherford: Fairleigh Dickinson University Press, 1971), 198.

17. Ruth Wilson, "Brideshead Reconsidered, II," *Quadrant* 226 (September 1982):63–65. This is a reply to Edward Pearce's 1982 *Encounter* article. Prufer, "The Death of Charm," 289.

18. Lawrence O'Toole, "Outbreak of Waugh: Two Views," *Film Comment* 18 (March–April 1982):78.

19. *Noblesse Oblige*, ed. Nancy Mitford (New York: Harper, 1956).

20. A letter described in Robert Murray Davis, *A Catalogue of the Evelyn Waugh Collection at the Humanities Research Center, the University of Texas at Austin* (Troy, N.Y.: Whitston Publishing Co., 1981), item E429, 20 June 1944.

21. The "Memorandum" reprinted, with minor errors in transcription, in Heath, "The Critics and the Memorandum."

22. For a discussion of the theology of deathbed repentance, see Paul Elmen, "*Brideshead Revisited:* A Twitch upon the Thread," *Christian Century* 99 (26 May 1982):630–31.

23. This is only the barest outline of a body of belief and practice that

had evolved over nearly two thousand years. Paul A. Doyle's *A Reader's Companion to the Novels and Short Stories of Evelyn Waugh* (Norman, Okla.: Pilgrim Books, 1989) is an indispensable guide for religious and all other allusions that are not clear from context.

24. See Hardy, "God, Man, and Others."

25. *Vile Bodies* (Boston: Little, Brown, 1977), 314. The novel was first published in 1930.

26. See Doyle, *Reader's Guide,* and the often reprinted discussion of the motif by Erwin Panofsky, "*Et in Arcadia Ego:* Poussin and the Elegiac Tradition," *Meaning in the Visual Arts: Papers in and on Art History* (Garden City, N.Y.: Doubleday Anchor Books, 1955), 295–320.

27. This image of the enchanted garden probably derives from Frances Hodgson Burnett's children's novel, *The Secret Garden,* in which a lively young girl helps to restore a motherless boy to physical and psychological health.

28. For a discussion of Waugh's changing attitude toward first person narration, see Robert Murray Davis, *Evelyn Waugh and the Forms of His Time* (Washington D.C.: Catholic University of America Press, 1989), chapter 13.

29. For the 1960 edition, page 98, Waugh revised this passage to emphasize the spiritual influence of Charles Ryder's mother and to anticipate Ryder's conversion.

30. Ford Madox Ford, *Joseph Conrad: A Personal Record* (New York: Octagon Books, 1971), 225, 182. First published in 1924.

31. For a discussion of Waugh's revision of Blanche's dialogue and setting, see Robert Murray Davis, *Evelyn Waugh, Writer* (Norman, Okla.: Pilgrim Books, 1981):131–38.

32. See Paul Fussell, *The Great War and Modern Memory* (New York: Oxford University Press, 1975), for a thorough and eloquent discussion of this issue.

33. For a good discussion of the presentation of alcoholism in the novel, see Thomas B. Gilmore, *Equivocal Spirits: Alcoholism and Drinking in Twentieth-Century Literature* (Chapel Hill: University of North Carolina Press; 1987), chapter 2, "*Brideshead Revisited:* Sebastian's Alcoholism as a Spiritual Illness," 36–47.

34. For a discussion of Waugh's recurrent theme of "imprisonment in the secular lush place," see Jeffrey Heath, "The Lush Places," *Evelyn Waugh Newsletter* 13 (Autumn 1979):5–8.

35. For a discussion of the history of the charge, see Hynes, "Varieties of Death Wish," and for a vigorous refutation of it, see Donald Greene, "A Partiality for Lords: Evelyn Waugh and Snobbery," *American Scholar* 58 (Summer 1989):444–59.

36. For a somewhat partial view on the subject, see Jacqueline A. Mc-Donnell, *Waugh on Women* (New York: St. Martin's Press, 1985).

37. For an excellent discussion of this theme, see Valentine Cunningham, *British Writers of the Thirties* (Oxford: Oxford University Press, 1988), especially chapter 3, "Destructive Elements."

Selected Bibliography

Primary Works

All of Waugh's novels were originally published in London by Chapman & Hall. All of his novels are now published in Boston by Little, Brown.

Black Mischief. London: Chapman & Hall, 1932; New York: Farrar & Rinehart, 1932.

Brideshead Revisited. London: Chapman & Hall, 1945; Boston: Little, Brown, 1946. Revised edition, London: Chapman & Hall, 1960.

The Diaries of Evelyn Waugh. Edited by Michael Davie. Boston: Little, Brown, n.d.

Decline and Fall. London: Chapman & Hall, 1928; Garden City, N.Y.: Doubleday, Doran, 1929.

The End of the Battle. Boston: Little, Brown, 1961. English title *Unconditional Surrender.*

The Essays, Articles and Reviews of Evelyn Waugh. Edited by Donat Gallagher. Boston: Little, Brown, 1984.

Evelyn Waugh, Apprentice. Edited by Robert Murray Davis. Norman, Okla.: Pilgrim Books, 1985.

A Handful of Dust. London: Chapman & Hall, 1934; New York: Farrar & Rinehart, 1934.

Helena. Boston: Little, Brown, 1950.

A Little Learning: An Autobiography: The Early Years. Boston: Little, Brown, 1964.

The Loved One. Boston: Little, Brown, 1948.

Men at Arms. Boston: Little, Brown, 1952.

Monsignor Ronald Knox. Boston: Little, Brown, 1959.

Officers and Gentlemen. Boston: Little, Brown, 1955.

The Ordeal of Gilbert Pinfold. Boston: Little, Brown, 1957.

Put Out More Flags. Boston: Little, Brown, 1942.

Rossetti: His Life and Works: London: Duckworth, 1928.

Scoop. Boston: Little, Brown, 1938.

Sword of Honour. Boston: Little, Brown, 1966. One-volume version of *Men at Arms, Officers and Gentlemen,* and *The End of the Battle.*

Vile Bodies. London: Chapman & Hall, 1930; New York: Jonathan Cape and Harrison Smith, 1930.

Secondary Works

Books

Bradbury, Malcolm. *Evelyn Waugh*. Edinburgh and London: Oliver & Boyd, 1964. Writers and Critics Series. Brief introduction.

Brideshead Revisited: An Eleven-Part Series for Television Adapted from the Novel by Evelyn Waugh. Manchester: Granada Television 1981. Designed to promote and explain the series, this book contains useful material about the background of the novel and its composition.

Carens, James F. *The Satiric Art of Evelyn Waugh*. Seattle: University of Washington Press, 1964.

Cook, William J., Jr. *Masks, Modes, and Morals: The Art of Evelyn Waugh*. Rutherford, N.J.: Fairleigh Dickinson University Press, 1971. The most thorough study of point of view and narrative persona in Waugh's novels.

Critical Essays on Evelyn Waugh. Edited by James F. Carens. Boston: G. K. Hall, 1987.

Davis, Robert Murray. *Evelyn Waugh and the Forms of His Time*. Washington, D.C.: Catholic University of America Press, 1989. Places Waugh in the context of his immediate fictional predecessors and contemporaries.

———. *Evelyn Waugh, Writer*. Norman, Okla.: Pilgrim Books, 1981. Traces Waugh's process of composition in his novels.

Doyle, Paul A. *Evelyn Waugh: A Critical Essay*. Grand Rapids, MI: William B. Eerdmans, 1969. Brief introduction by the leading American student of Waugh's work.

———. *A Reader's Companion to the Novels and Short Stories of Evelyn Waugh*. Norman, Okla.: Pilgrim Books, 1989. Explains allusions and identifies characters. An essential work.

Evelyn Waugh: The Critical Heritage. Edited by Martin Stannard. London and Boston: Routledge by Kegan Paul, 1984. Reprints reviews of Waugh's books; useful for historical perspective.

Heath, Jeffrey. *The Picturesque Prison: Evelyn Waugh and His Writing*. Kingston and Montreal: McGill-Queen's University Press, 1982. A provocative and essential study of Waugh that sometimes ignores the context of quotations in the pursuit of a thesis.

Littlewood, Ian. *The Writings of Evelyn Waugh.* Totowa, N.J.: Barnes & Noble, 1983. Good on local stylistic effects, but trivializes Waugh's themes and accomplishments.

Lodge, David. *Evelyn Waugh.* New York and London: Columbia University Press, 1971. An introductory, pamphlet-length study.

McDonnell, Jacqueline A. *Waugh on Women.* New York: St. Martin's Press, 1985. Hostile study that frequently ignores context, narrative strategy, and other elements of narrative art in pursuit of a thesis.

Stannard, Martin. *Evelyn Waugh: The Early Years 1903–1939.* New York: W. W. Norton, 1987. Better researched and more laboriously written than Sykes's biography.

Stopp, Frederick J. *Evelyn Waugh: Portrait of an Artist.* Boston: Little, Brown, 1958. Written with the cooperation of Waugh and his English publisher; more acute and better informed than most first studies and still very useful.

Sykes, Christopher. *Evelyn Waugh: A Biography.* Boston: Little, Brown, 1975. Authorized biography done by a friend with minimal research and even less critical insight.

Articles

See also the articles cited in notes 8–19. The most significant are cited here.

Delasanta, Rodney, and Mario L. D'Avanzo. "Truth and Beauty in *Brideshead Revisited.*" *Modern Fiction Studies* 11 (1965):140–52.

Greene, Donald. "Peerage Nomenclature in *Brideshead Revisited.*" *Evelyn Waugh Newsletter* 16 (Autumn 1982): 5–6. Greene's thorough and erudite work on the physical and social background of Waugh's novels continues to appear in a variety of journals.

Heath, Jeffrey. "*Brideshead:* The Critics and the Memorandum." *English Studies* 56 (1975):222–30.

Hynes, Joseph. "Two Affairs Revisited." *Twentieth Century Literature* 33 (1987):234–53. Compares *Brideshead Revisited* and Graham Greene's *The End of the Affair.*

Prufer, Thomas. "The Death of Charm and the Advent of Grace: Waugh's *Brideshead Revisited.*" *Communio* 10 (1983):281–291. The most important recent study of the novel, treating reversals in character and structure.

Wooton, Carl. "Evelyn Waugh's *Brideshead Revisited:* War and Limited Hope." *Midwest Quarterly* 10 (1969):359–75.

Bibliographies

Davis, Robert Murray, Paul A. Doyle, Donat Gallagher, Charles E. Linck, and Winnifred M. Bogaards. *A Bibliography of Evelyn Waugh.* Troy, N.Y.: Whitston, 1986. Supersedes all previous bibliographies, including Davis et al., *Evelyn Waugh: A Checklist of Primary and Secondary Material,* 1972.

Davis, Robert Murray. *A Catalogue of the Evelyn Waugh Collection at the Humanities Research Center, the University of Texas at Austin.* Troy, N.Y.: Whitston, 1981. Describes manuscript and archival material; lists and summarizes a large collection of Waugh's letters, most of them to his literary agent.

Evelyn Waugh Newsletter. Edited by Paul A. Doyle since 1967, this publication contains useful critical and biographical articles on Waugh as well as a running bibliography of secondary work and an annual review of major critical works.

Index

Index

The Author

Robert Murray Davis has written or edited seven books and numerous articles on Evelyn Waugh, including a catalog of the major collection of his manuscripts and other materials, a bibliography, and two critical books; other books and articles on modern English and American fiction and the literature of the American West; and poetry and personal essays.

A professor of English at the University of Oklahoma, he has served as visiting lecturer in Canada and in Europe.